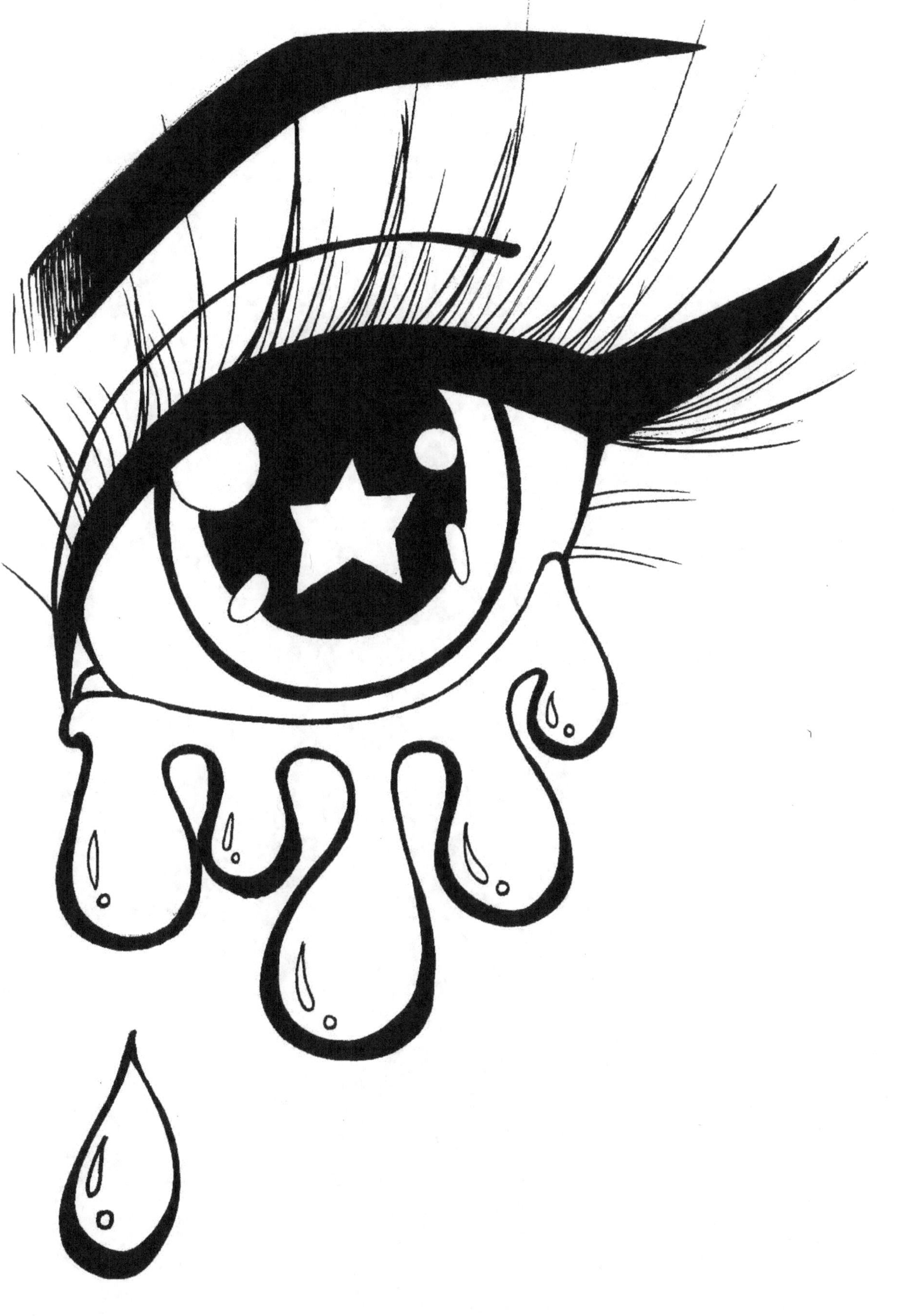

Illustrious by Akeem Wayne Presents:

The Beat

Painting Faces

I have the honor of knowing a few extremely talented Makeup Artists and what they do heavily influences my artwork, so this coloring book is dedicated to all the talented makeup artists out there because what you are doing is art, and it has huge impact on our culture. A lot of makeup artists use face charts to create looks, and I wanted to create a coloring book that blended the art of makeup with pop surrealist art. Use this Coloring book to create looks, practice techniques, or just have fun and relax.

— Akeem Wayne

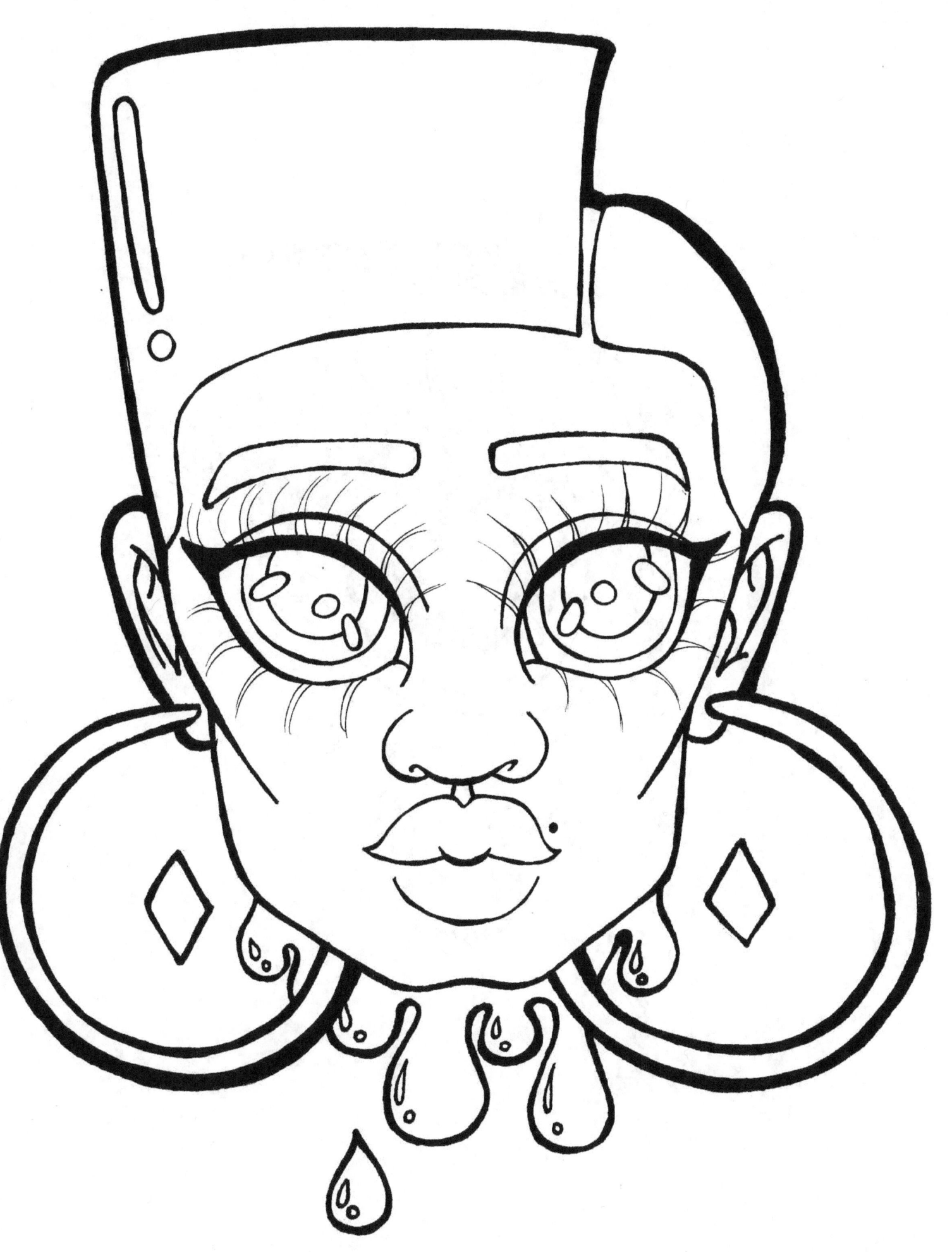

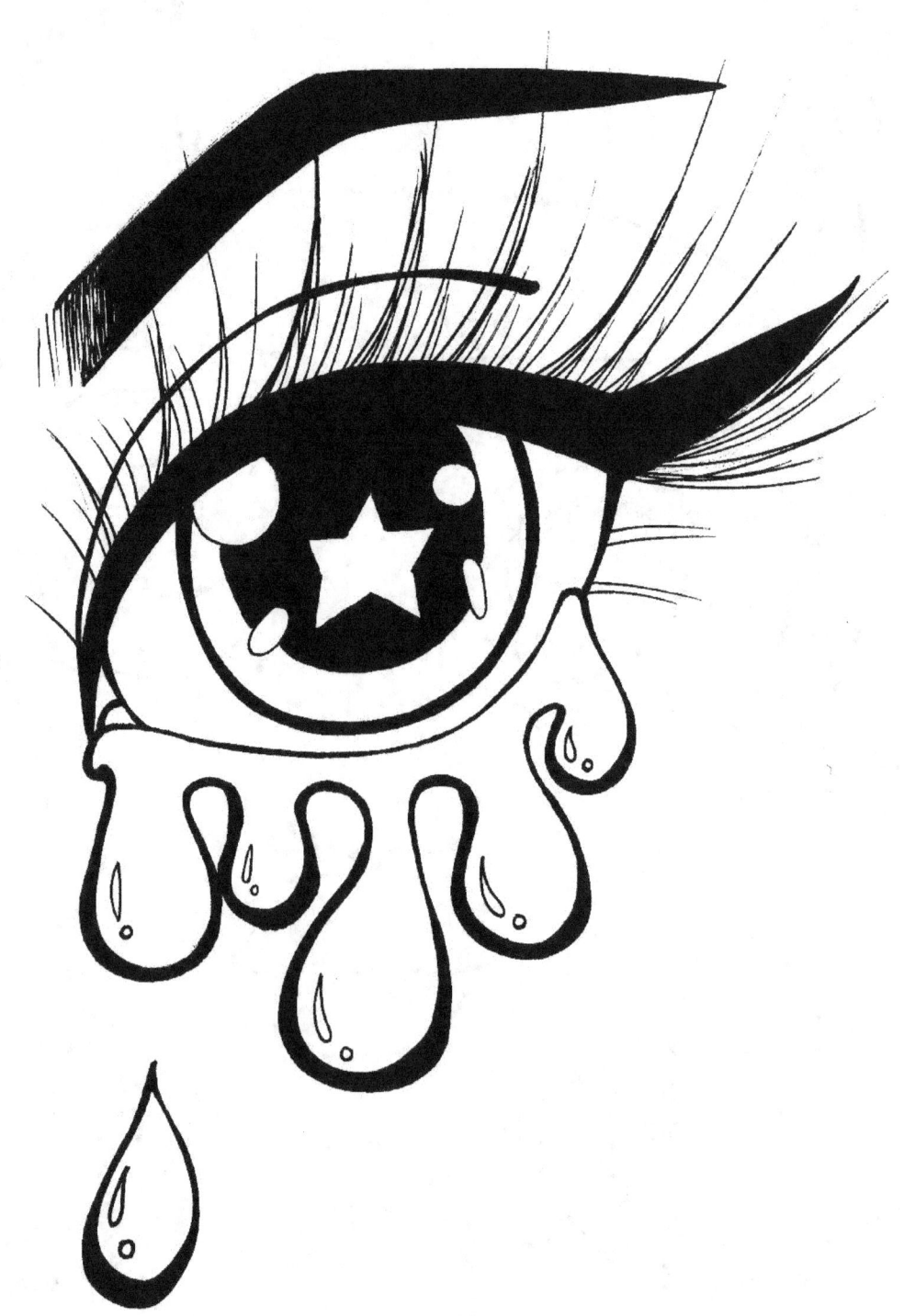

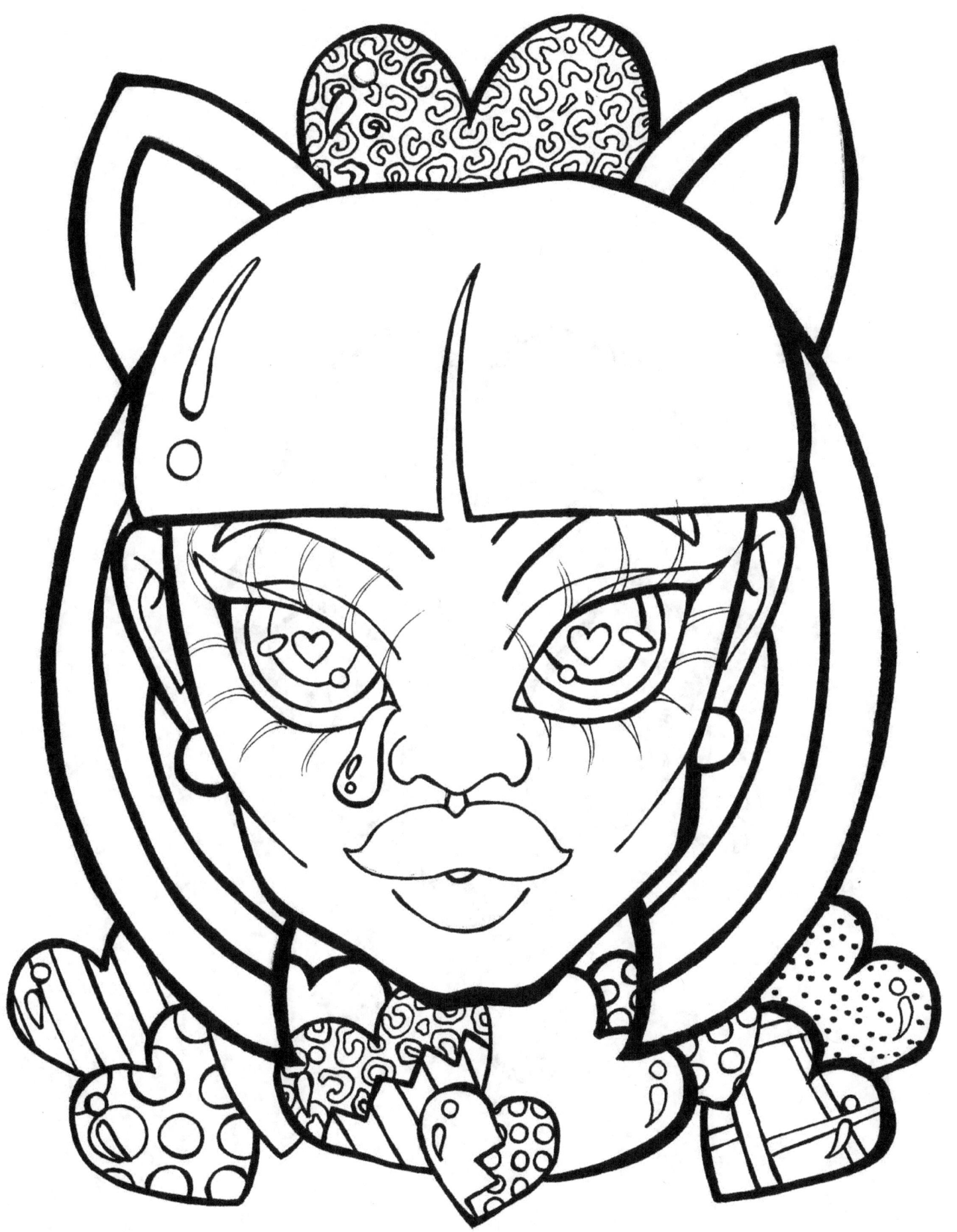

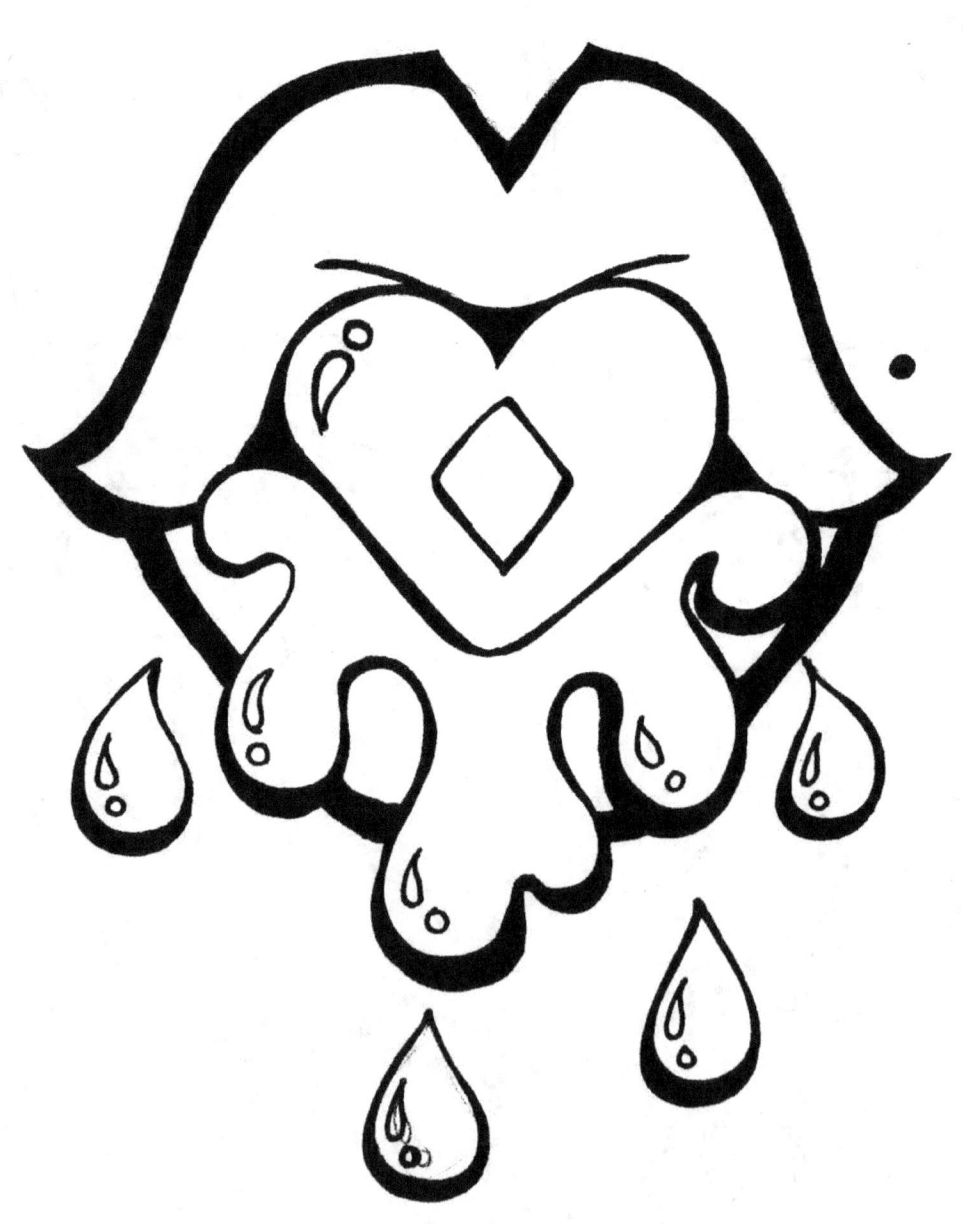

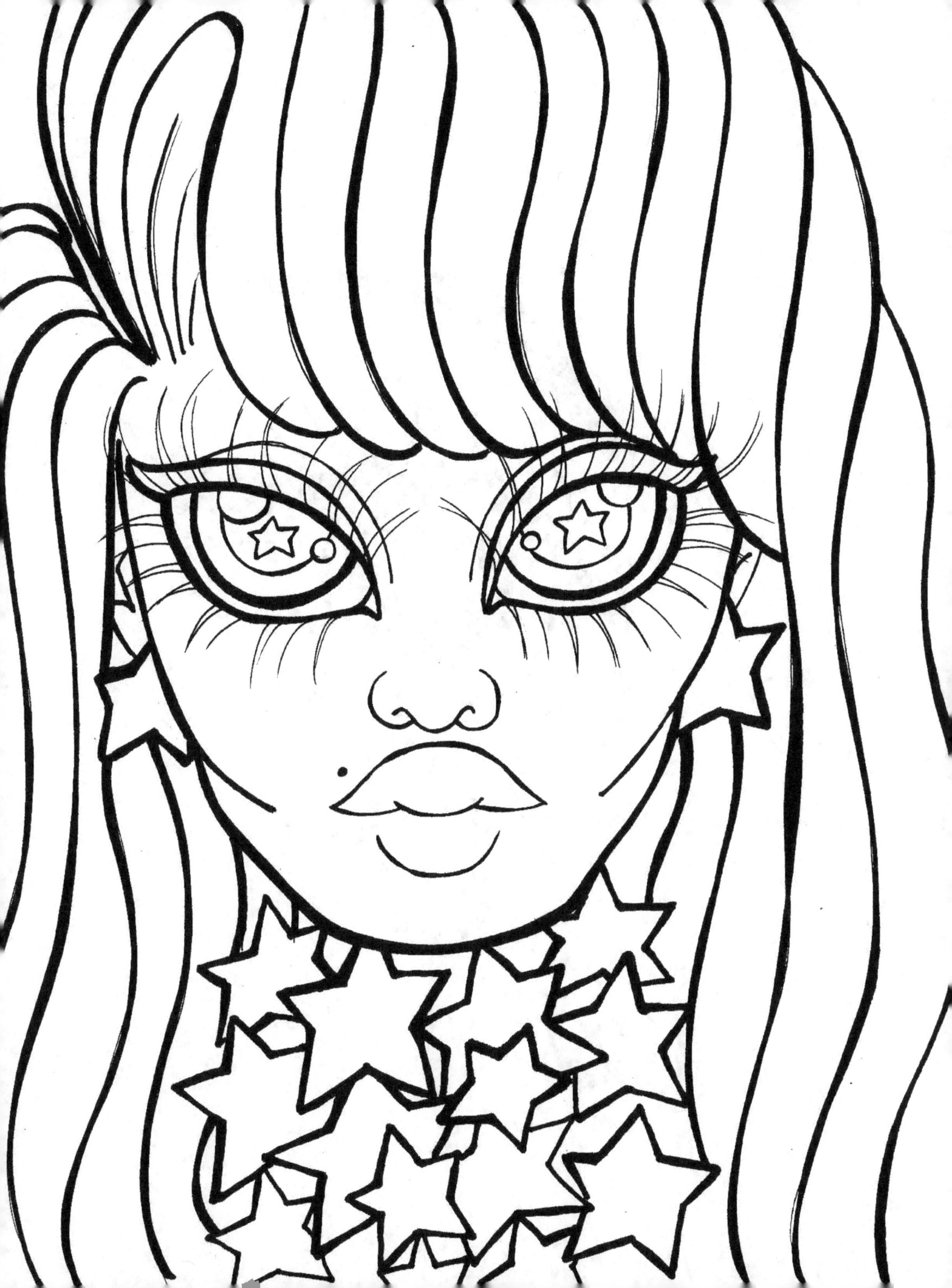

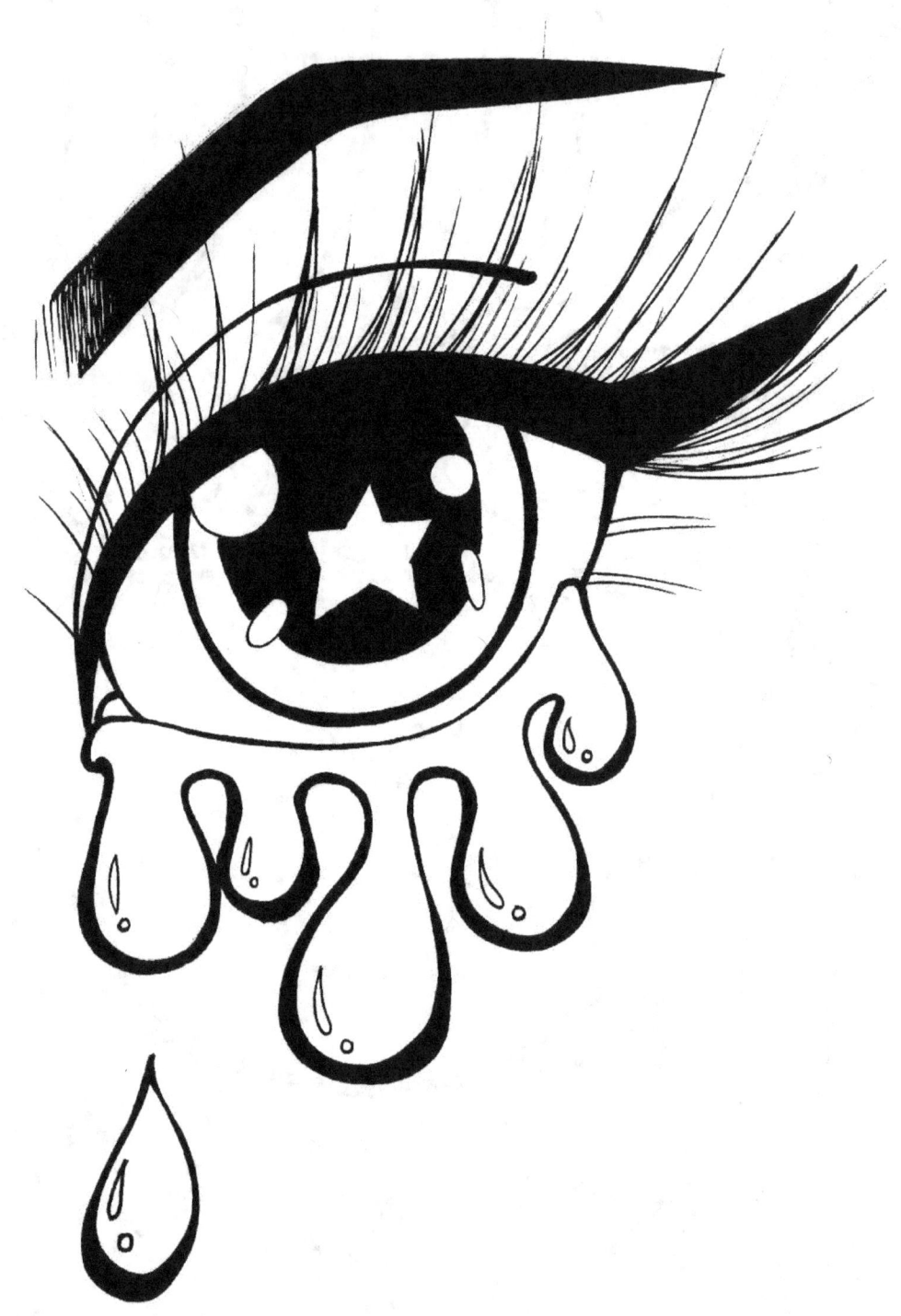

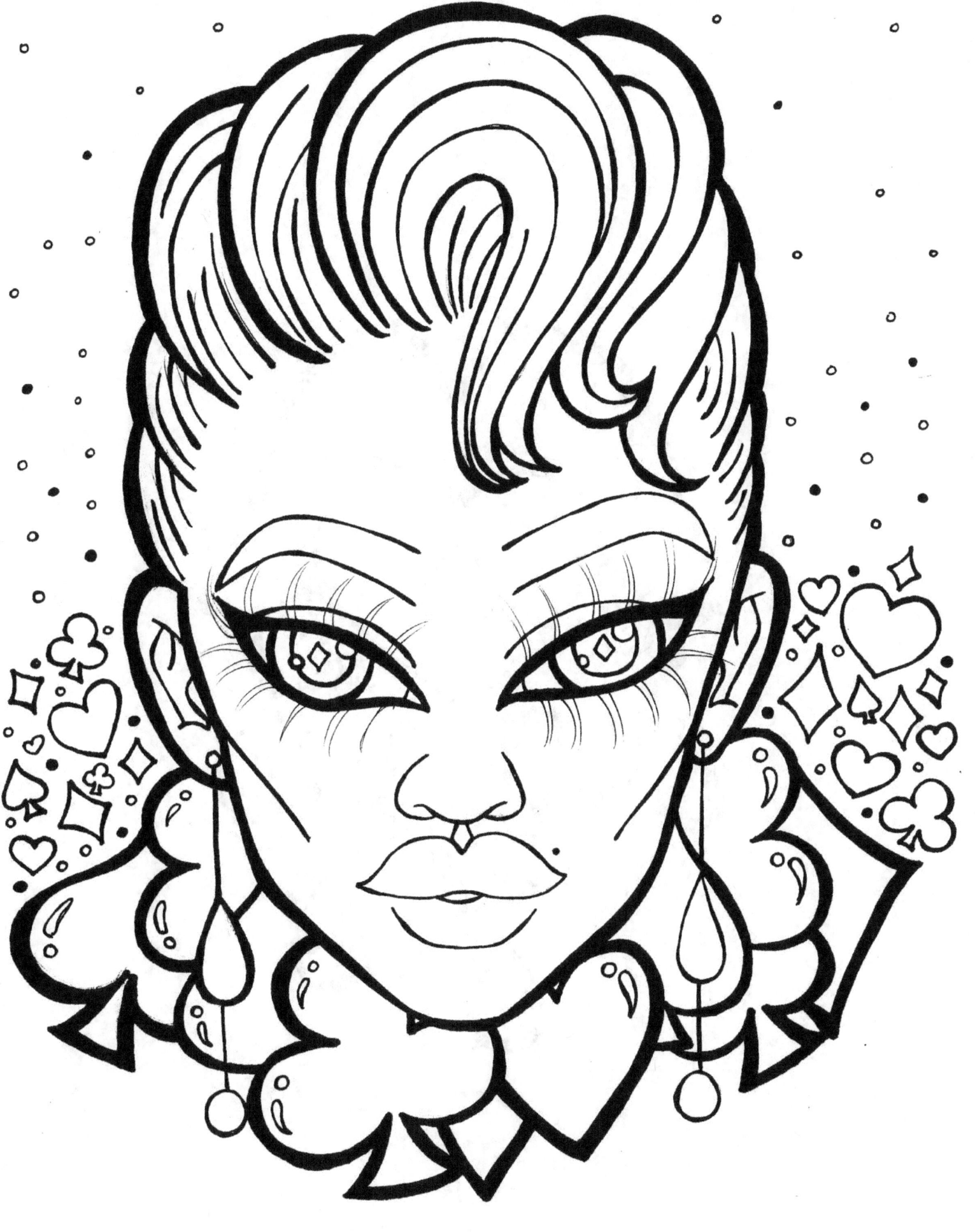

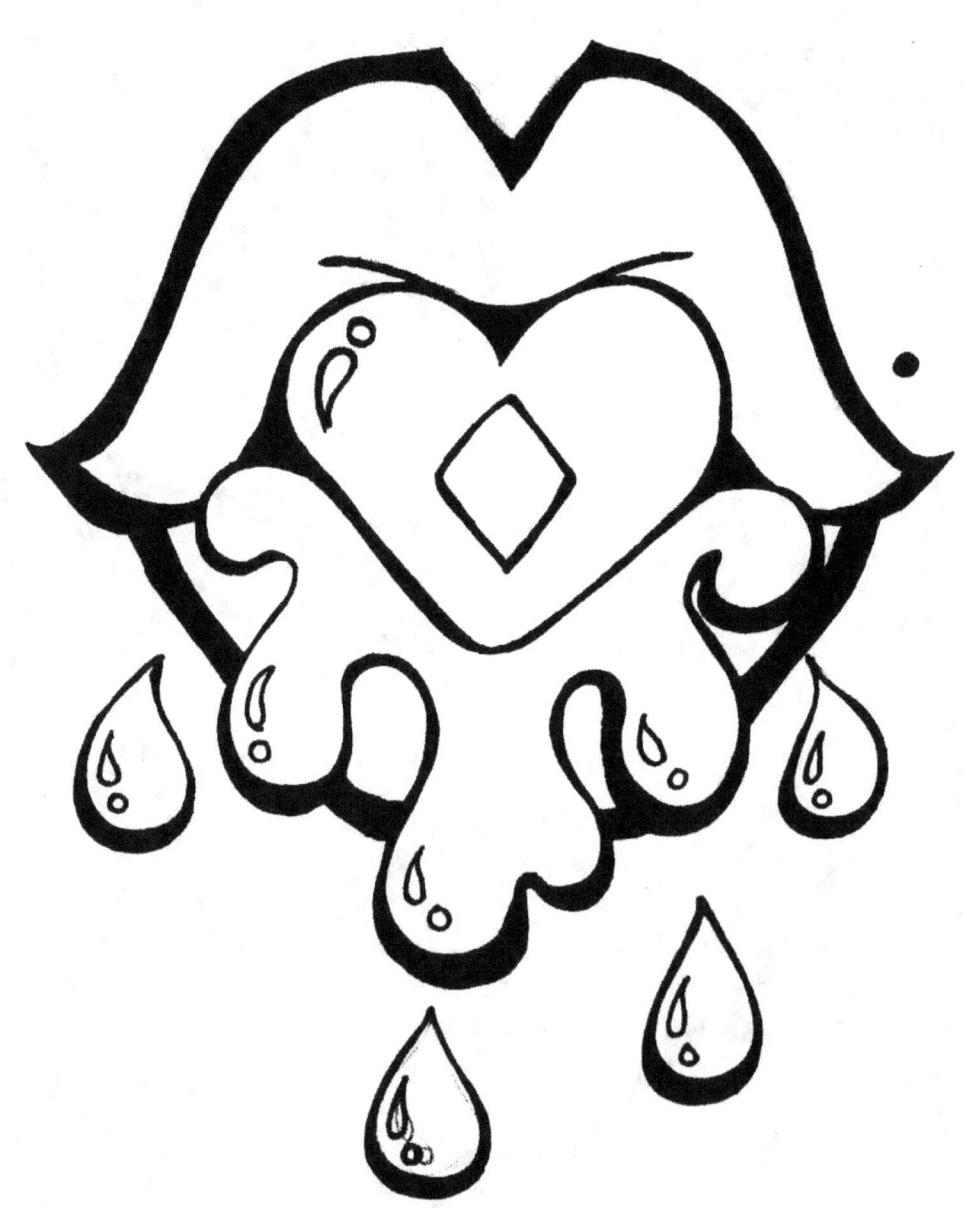

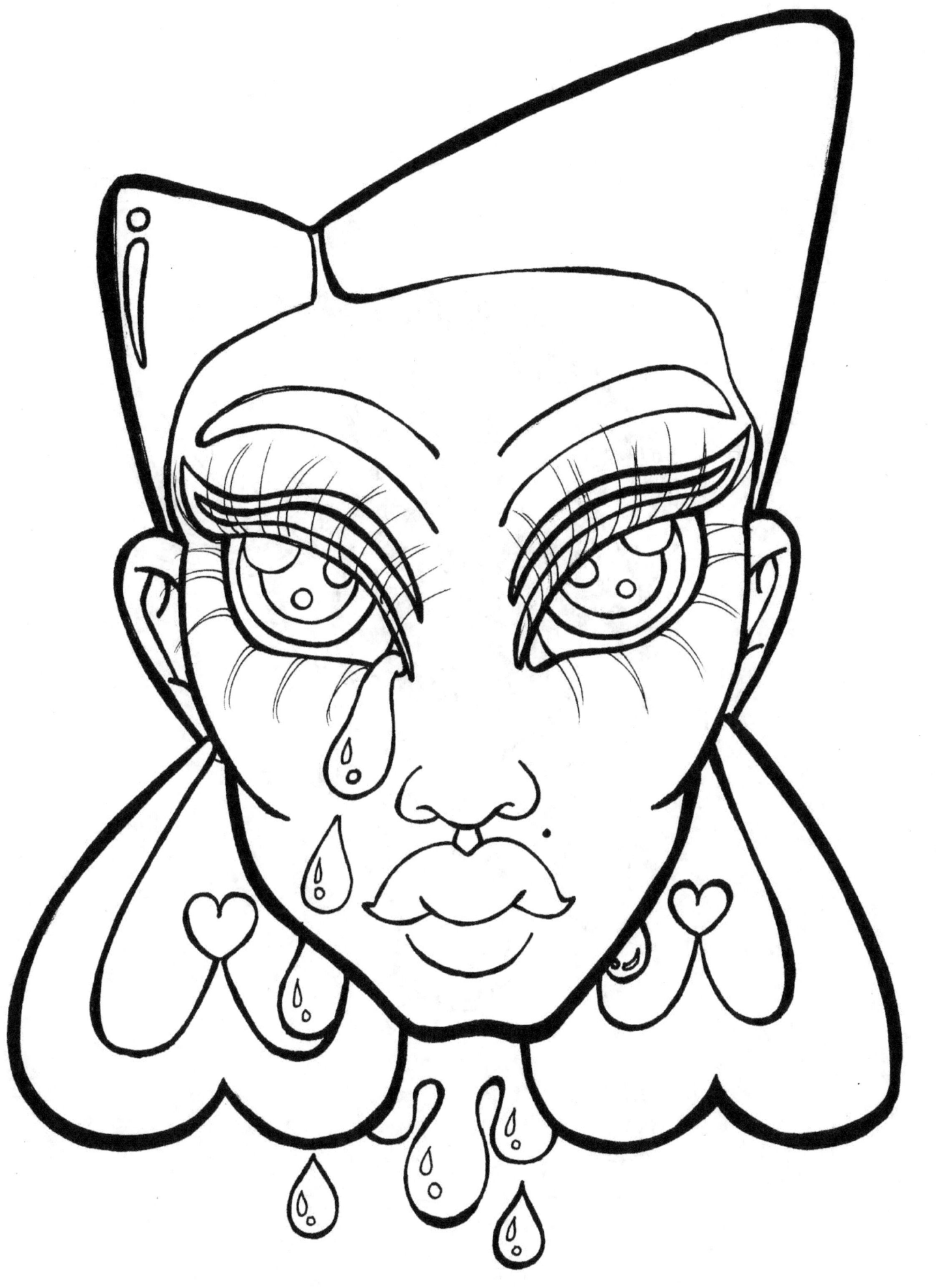

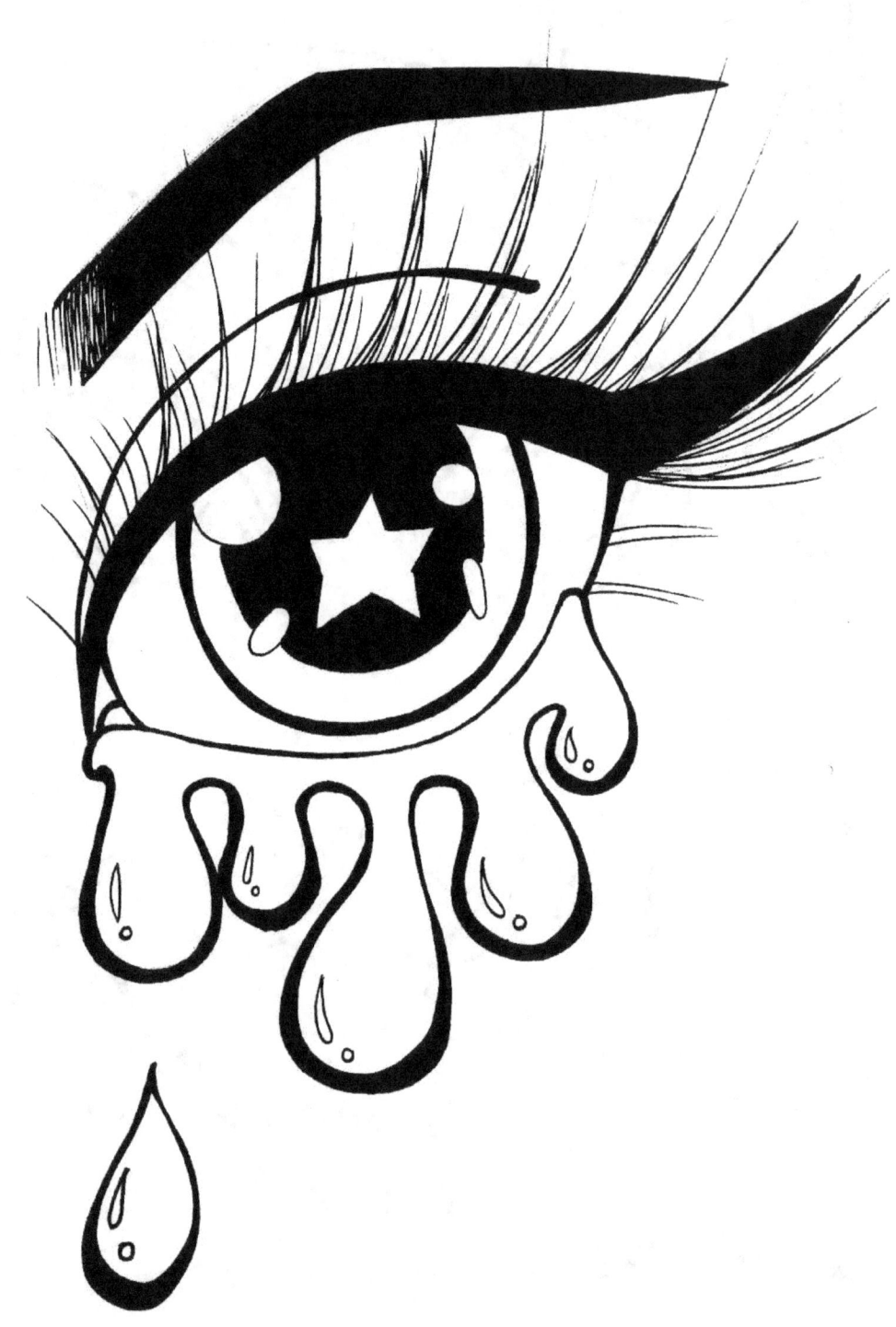

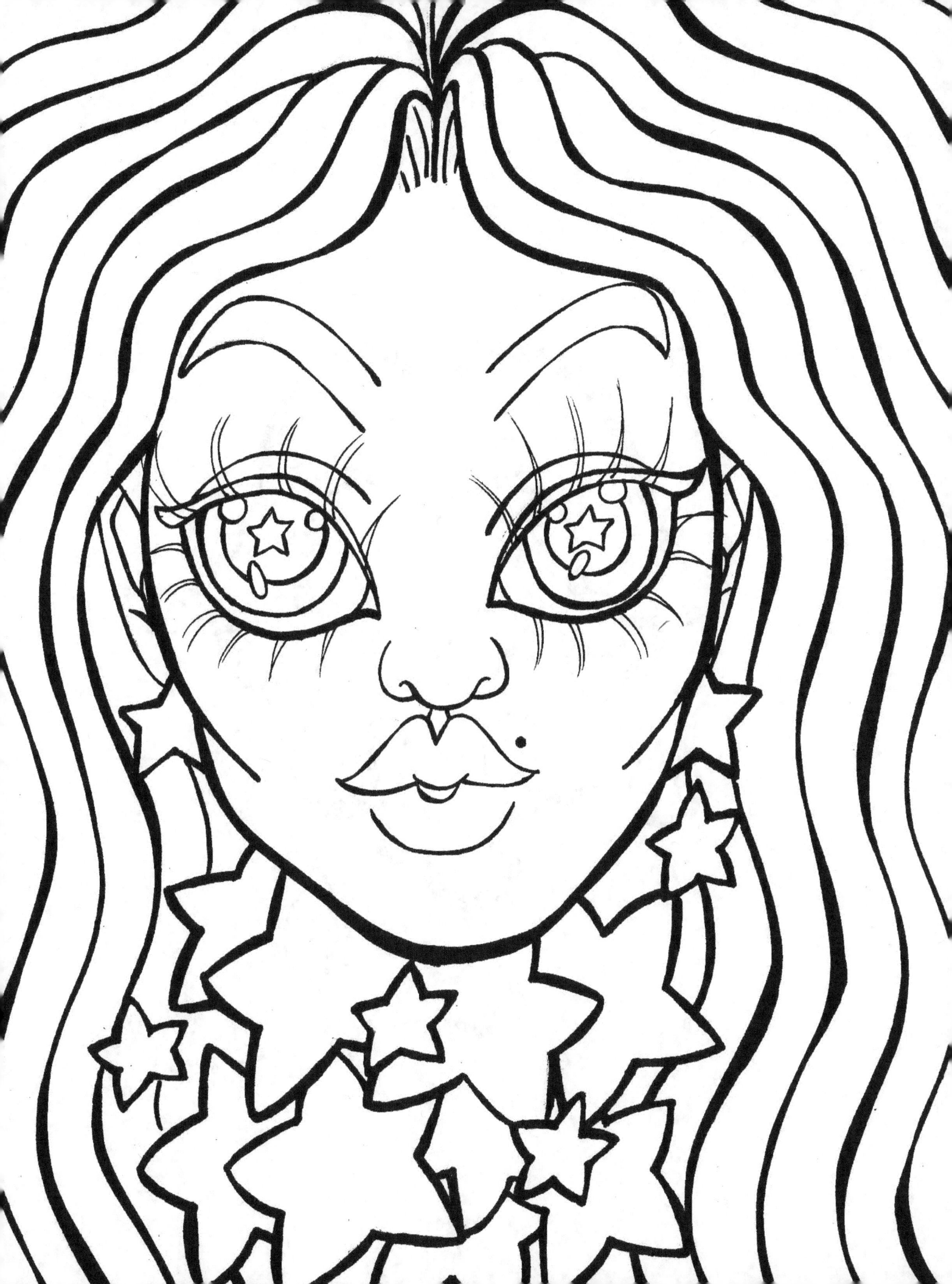

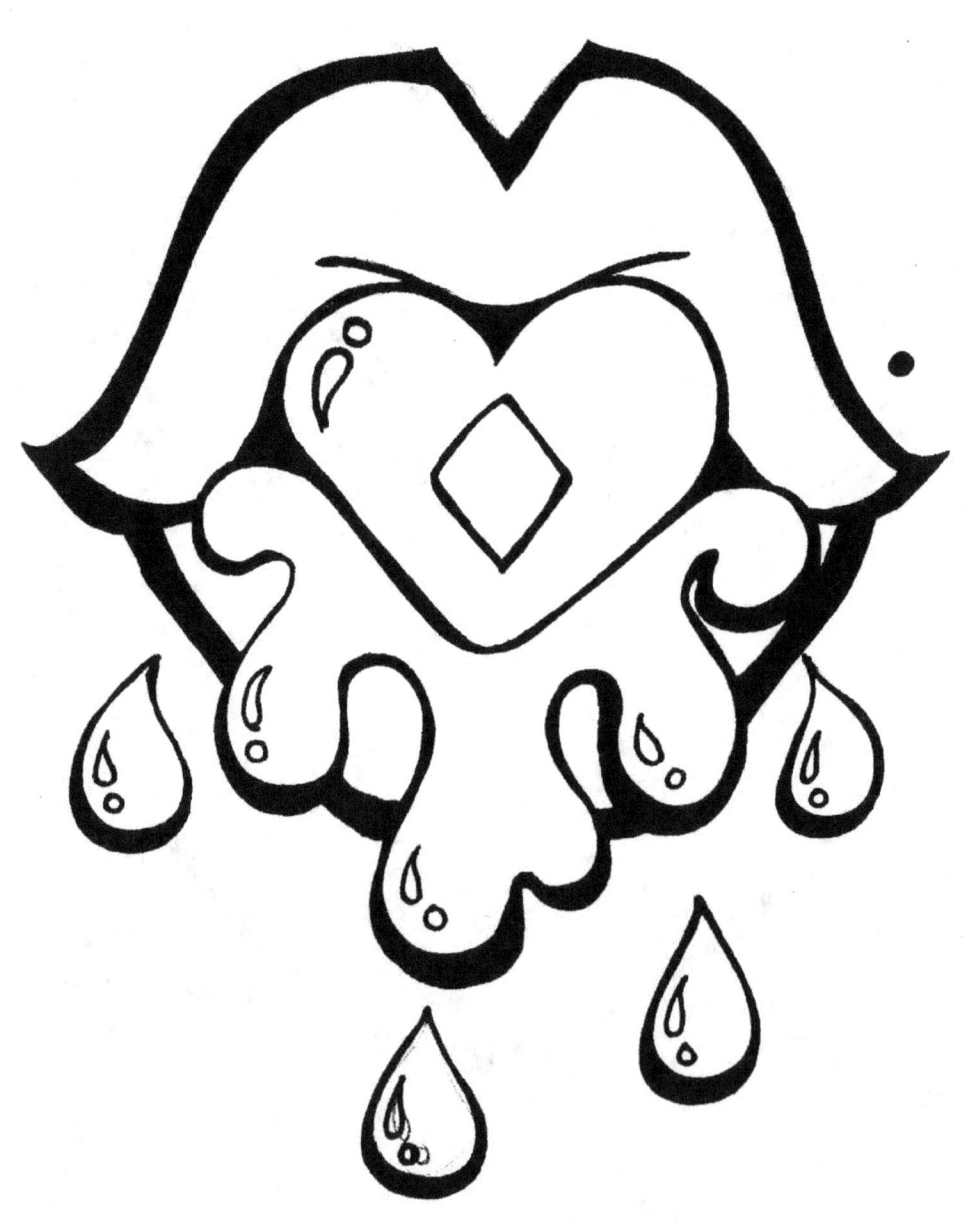

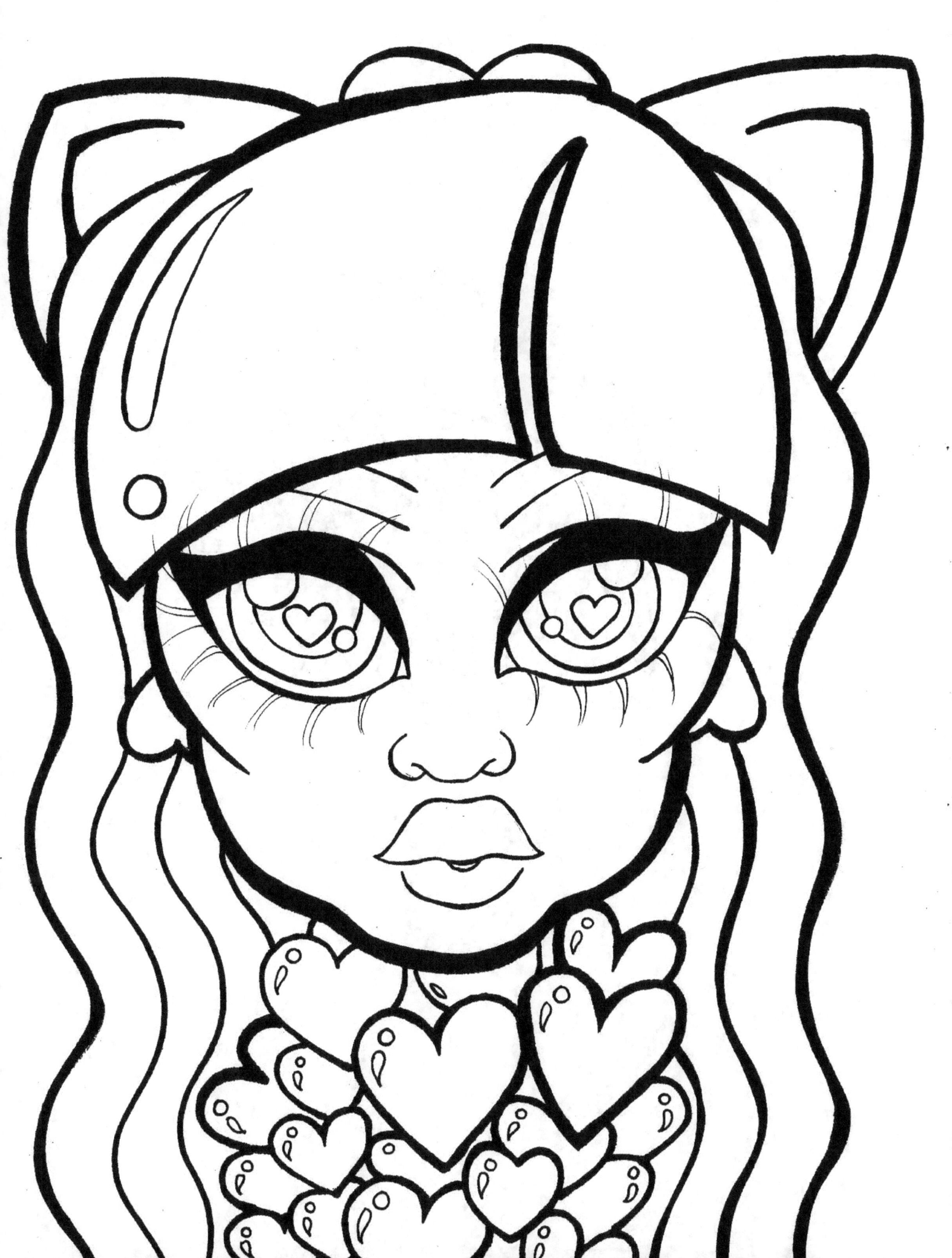

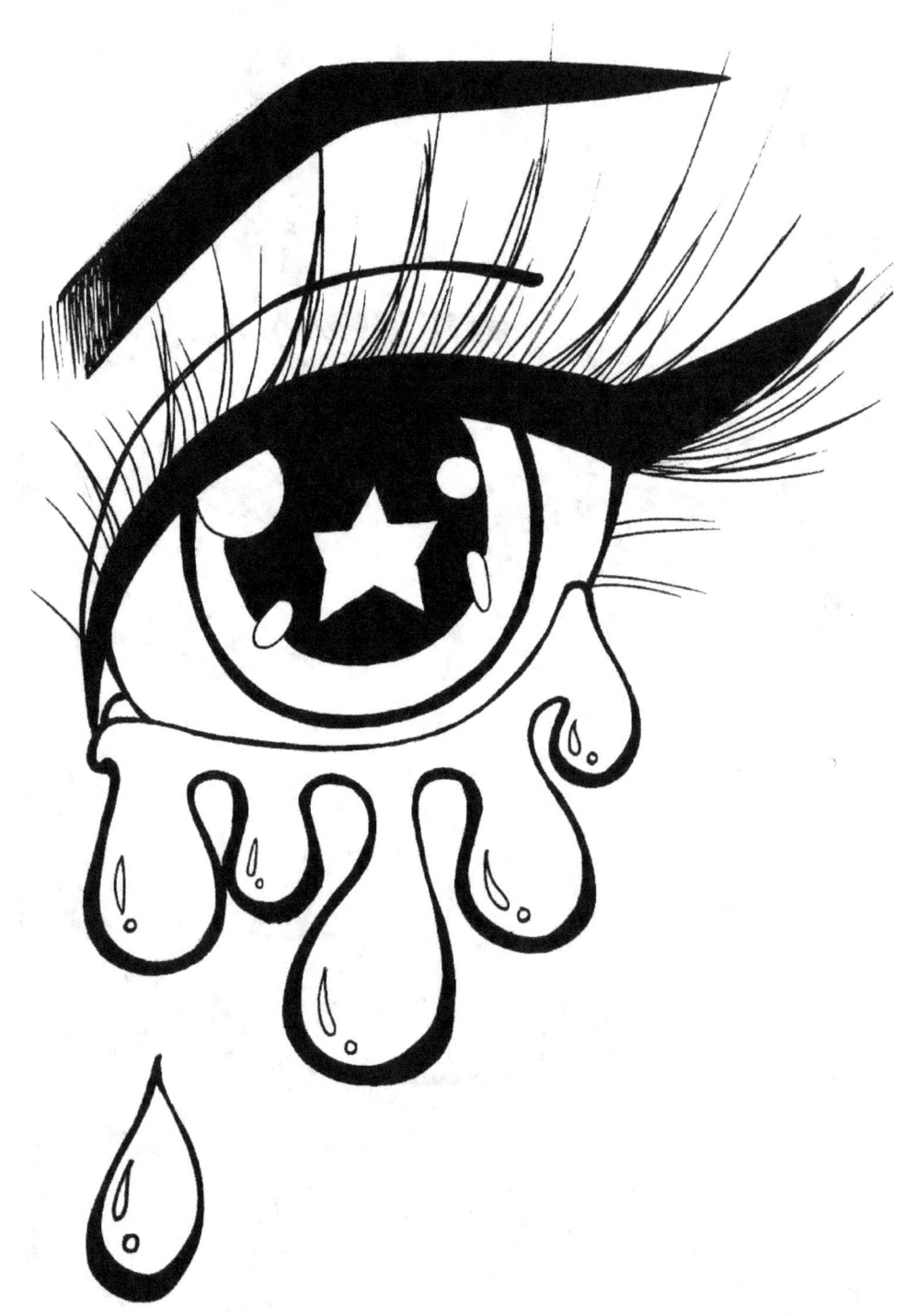

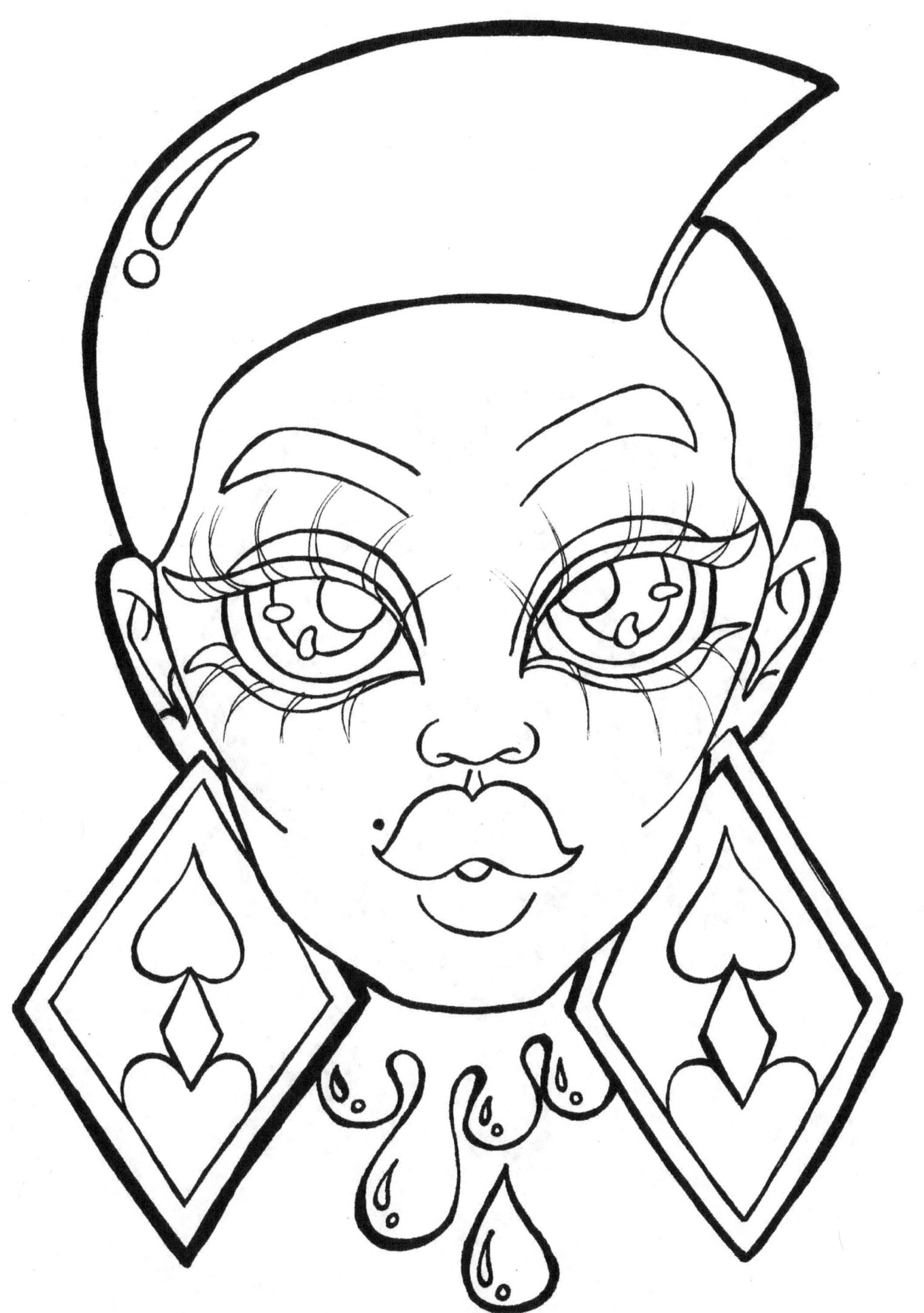

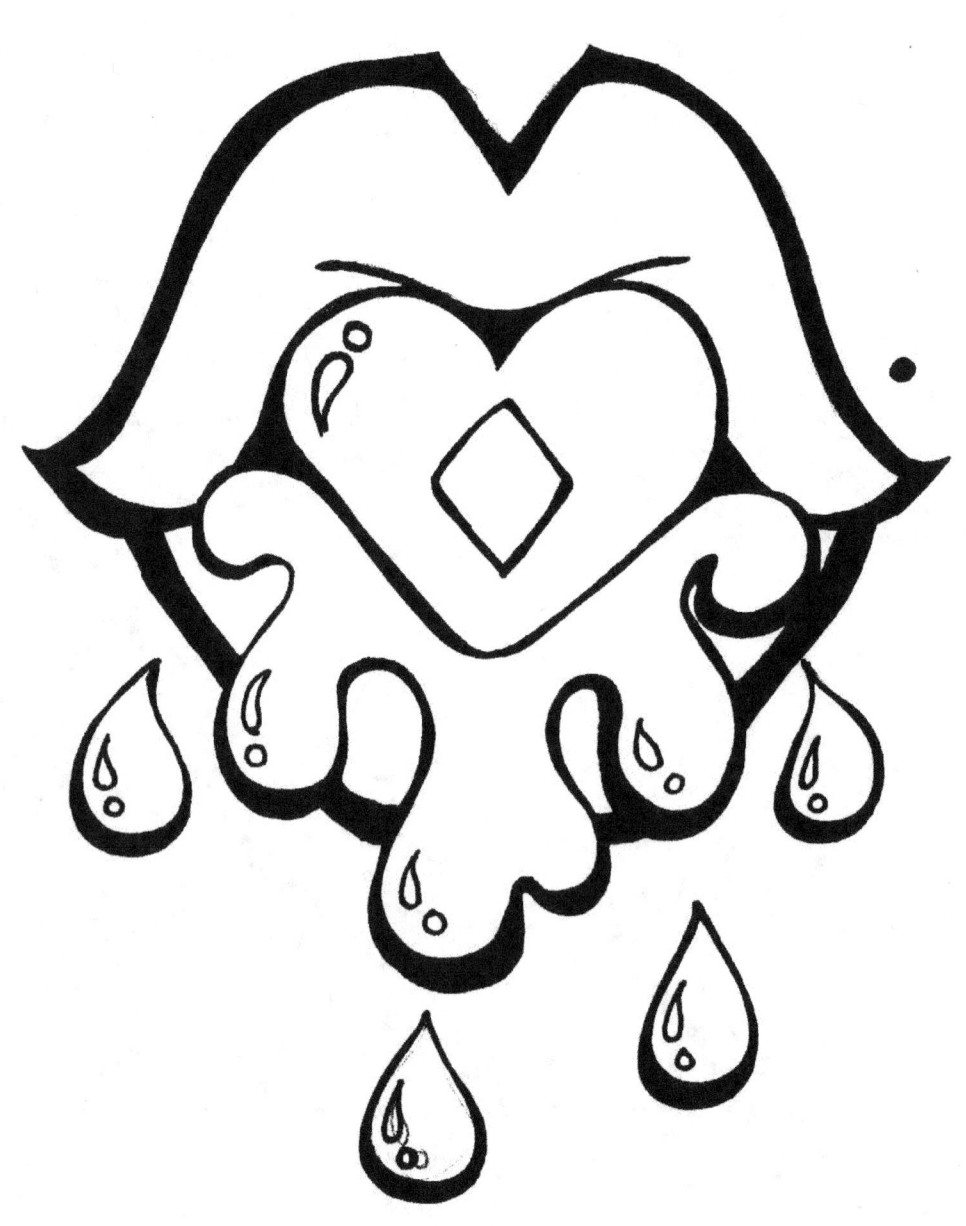

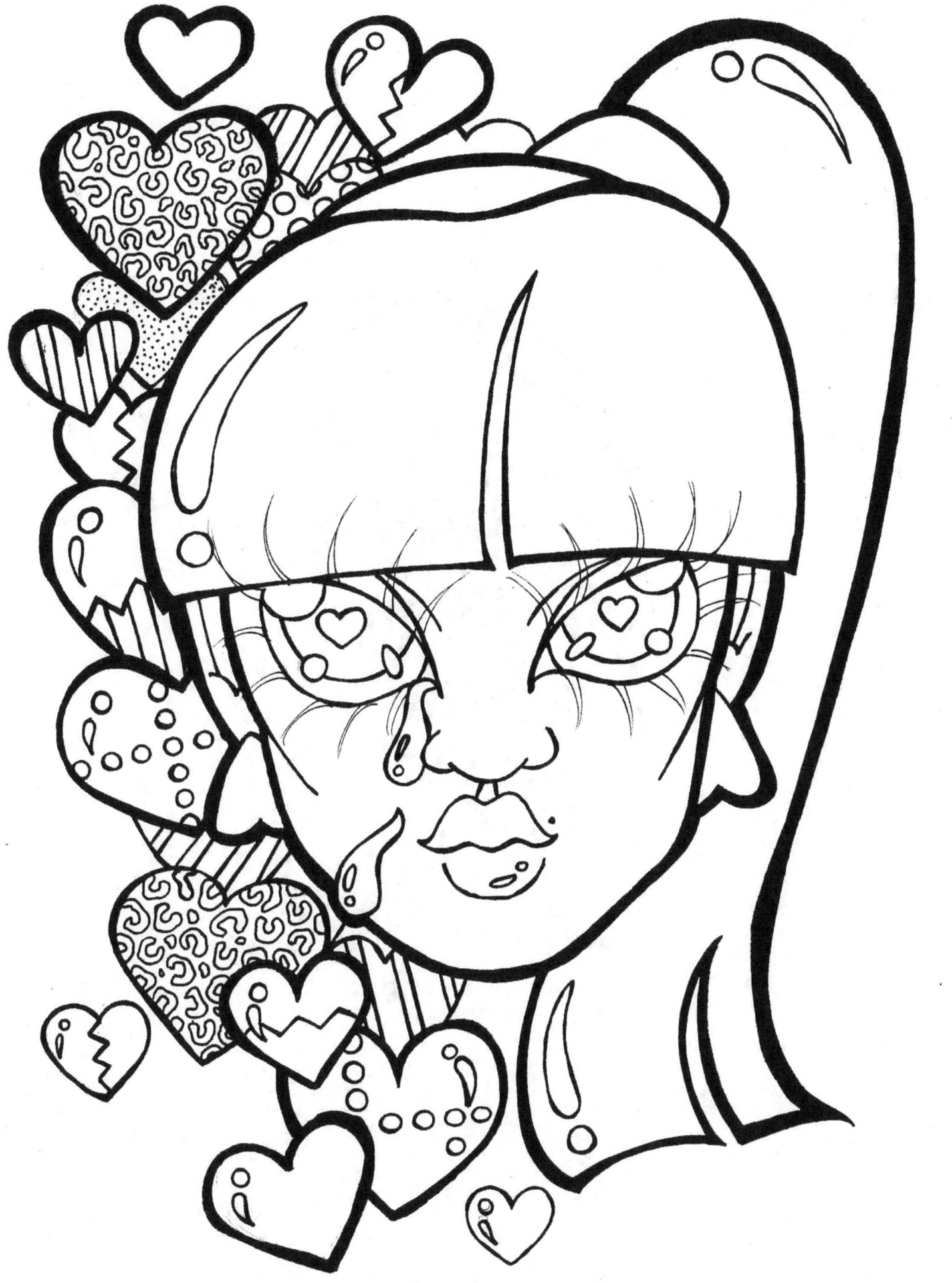

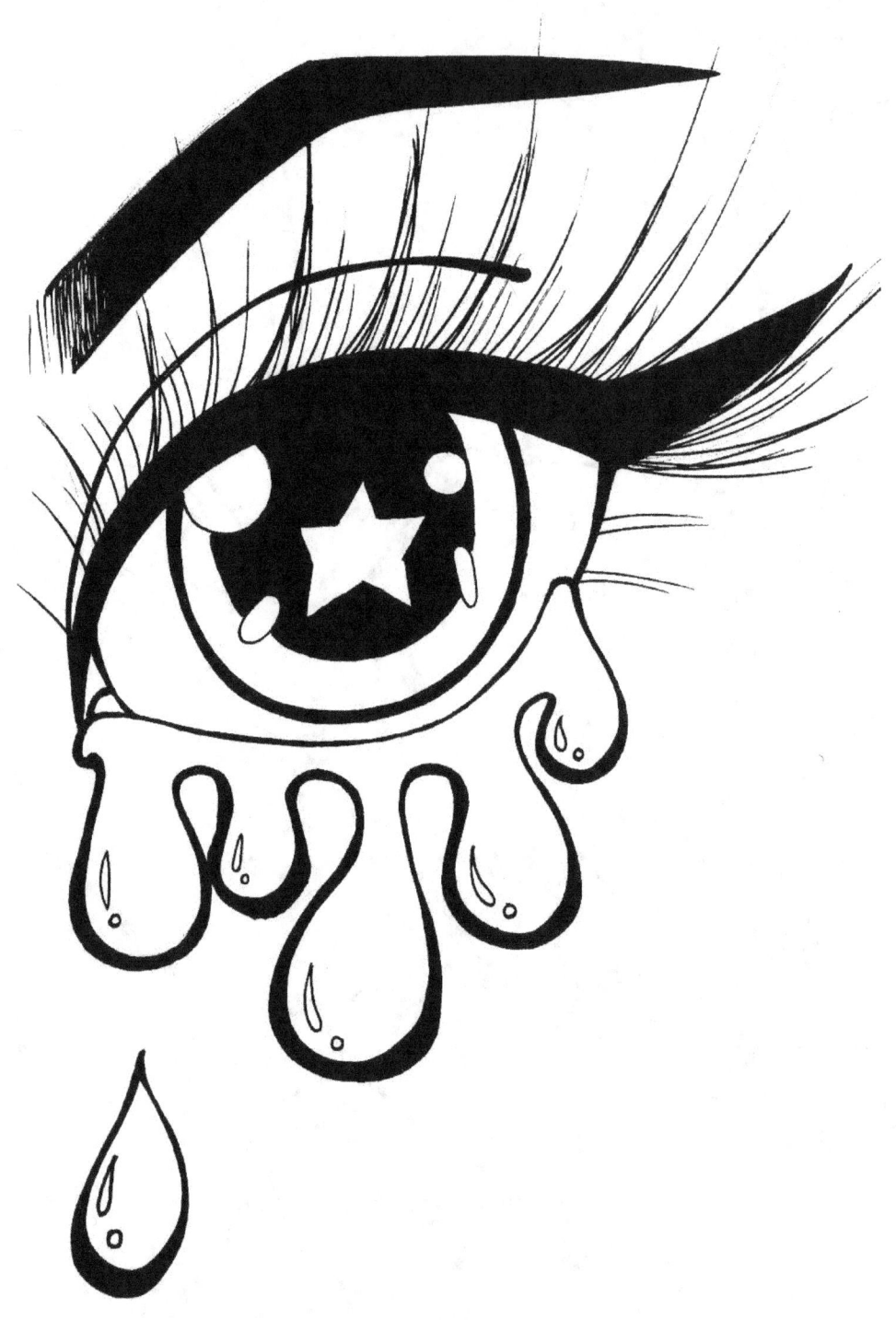

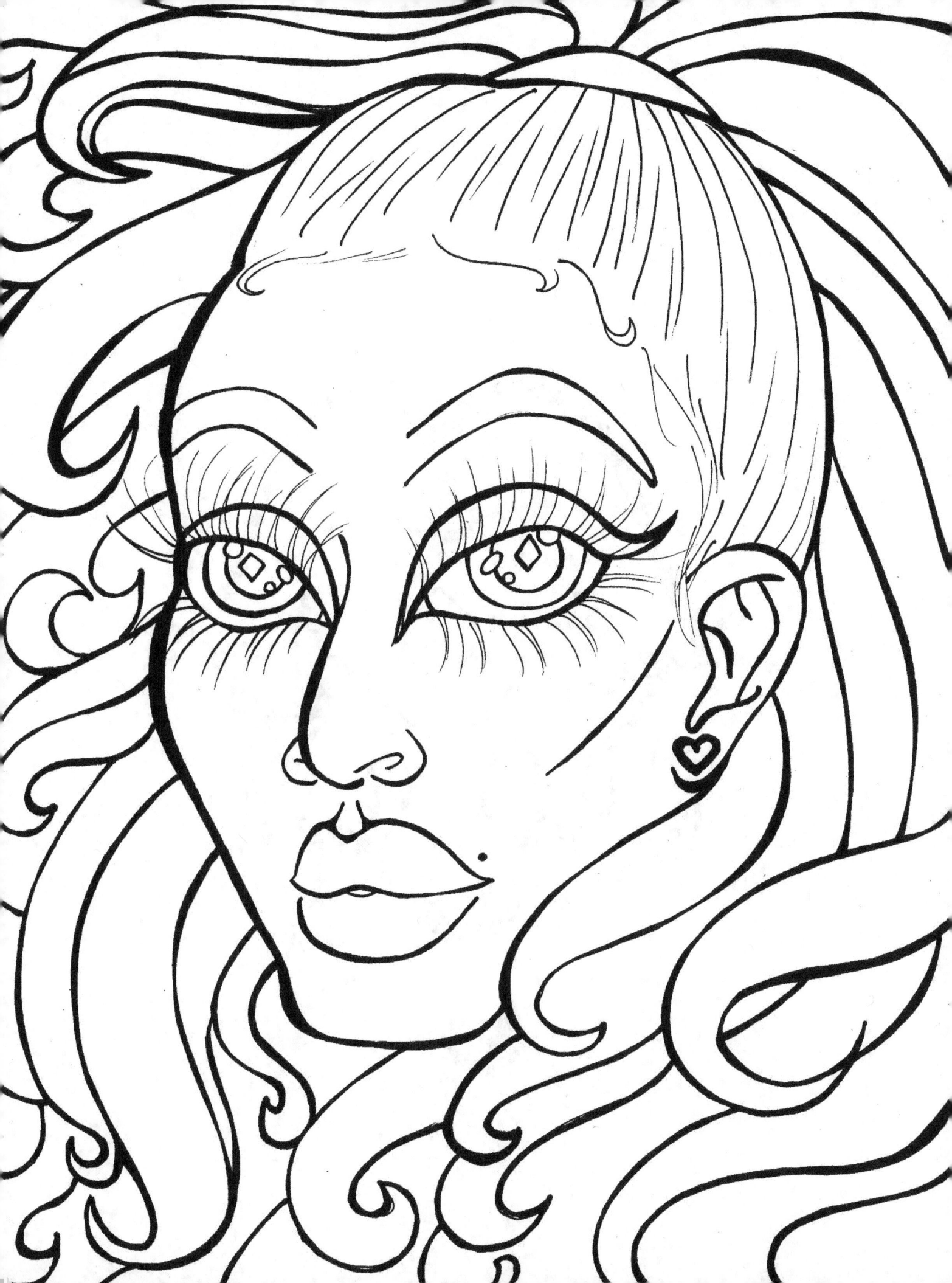

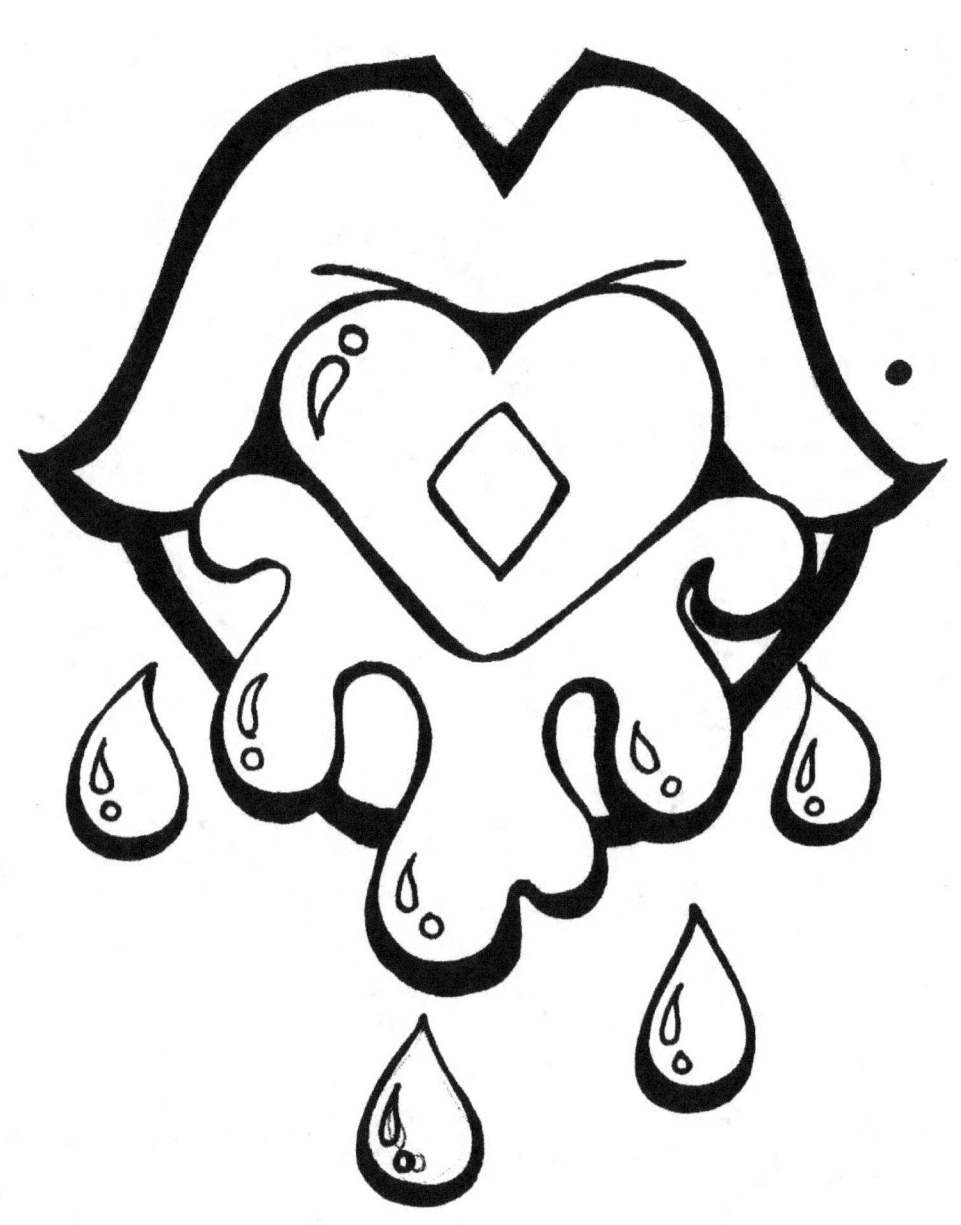

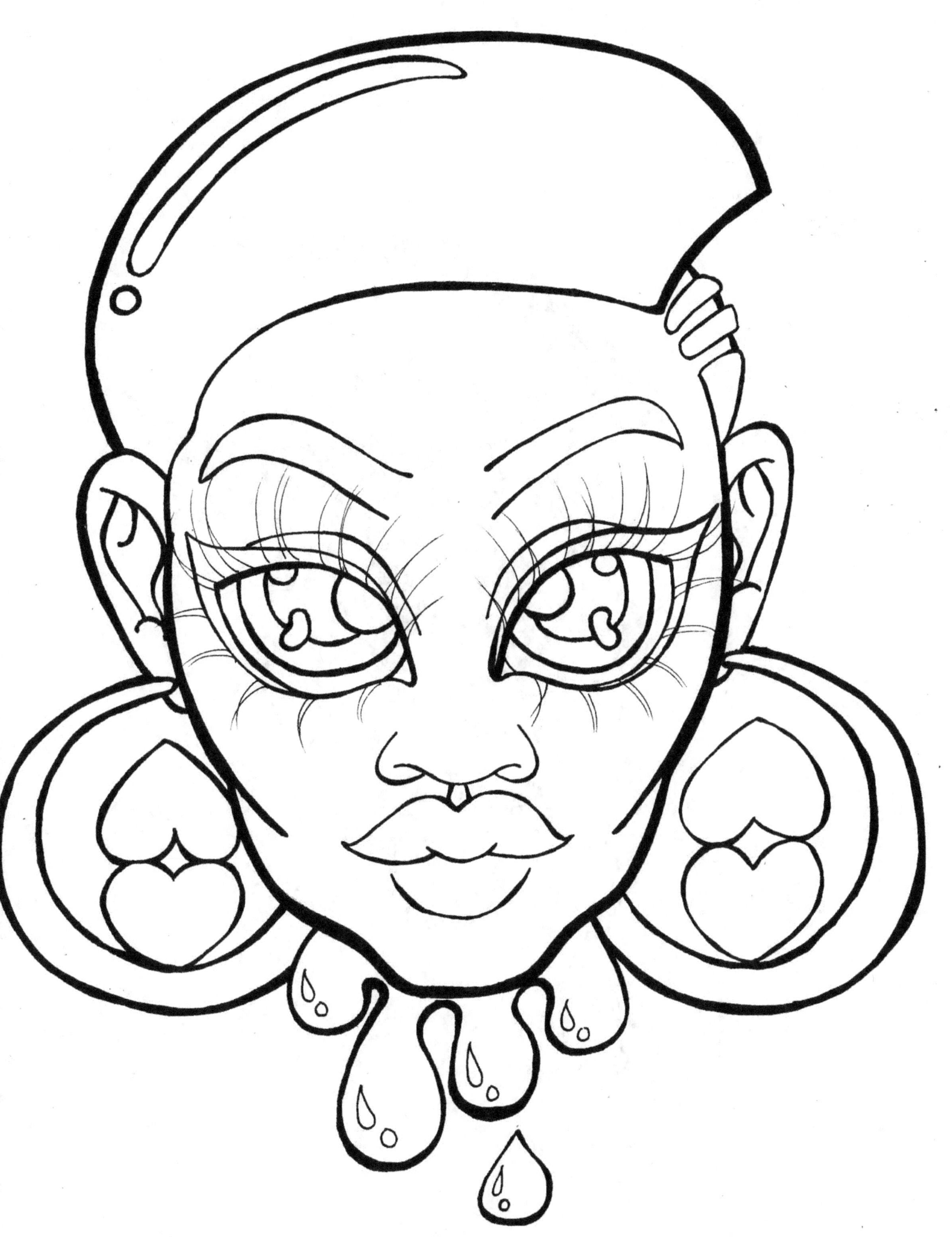

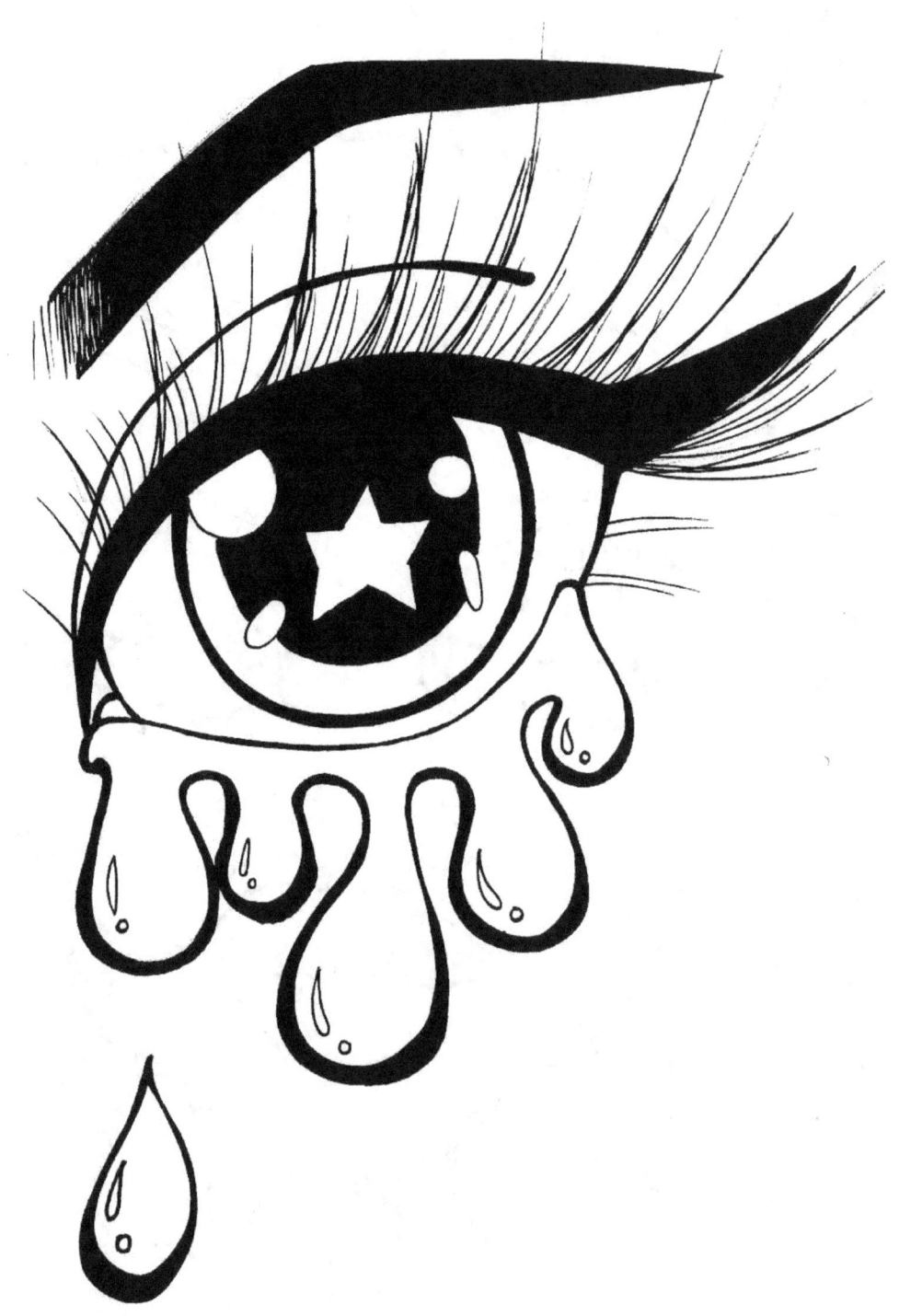

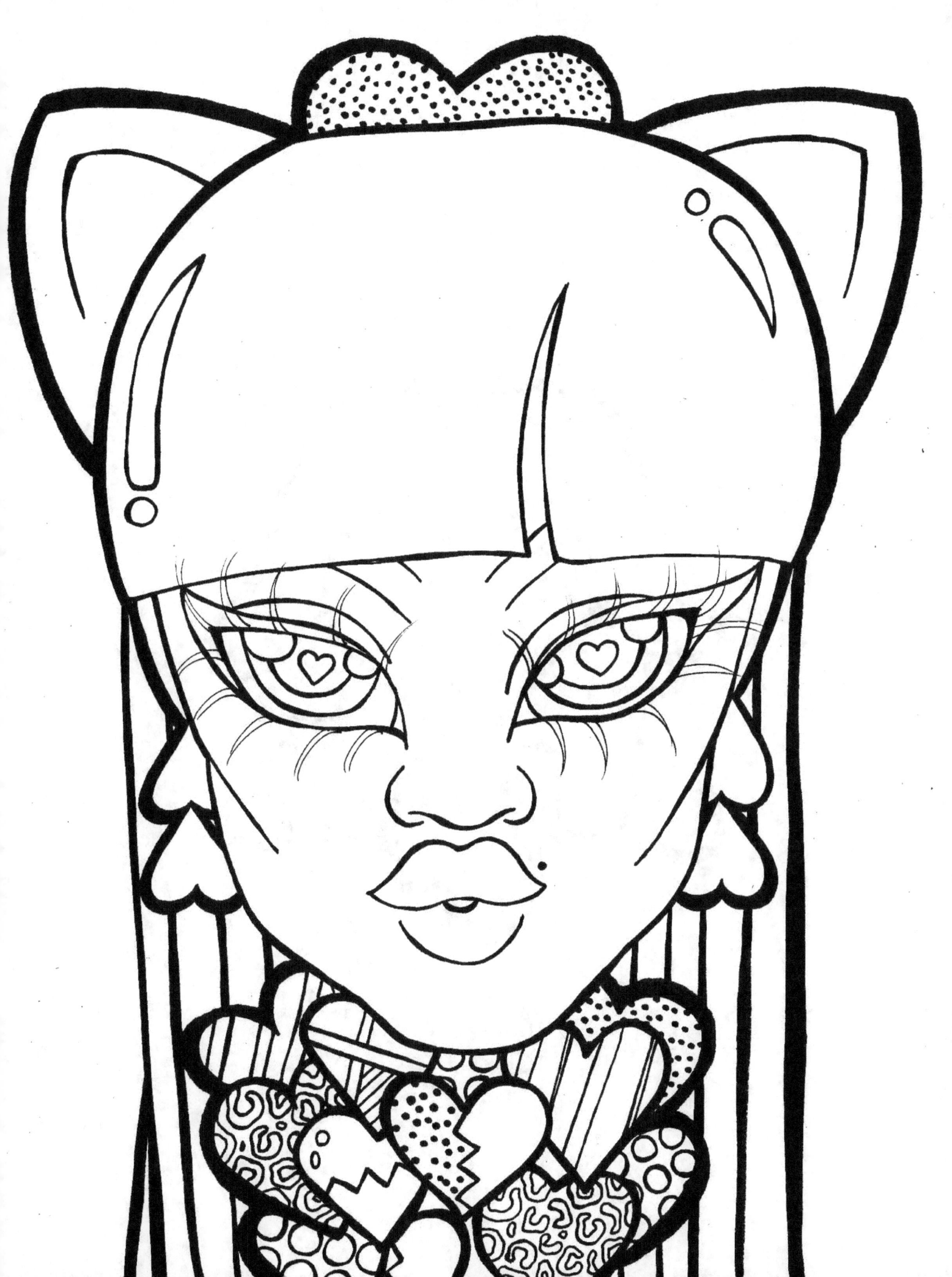

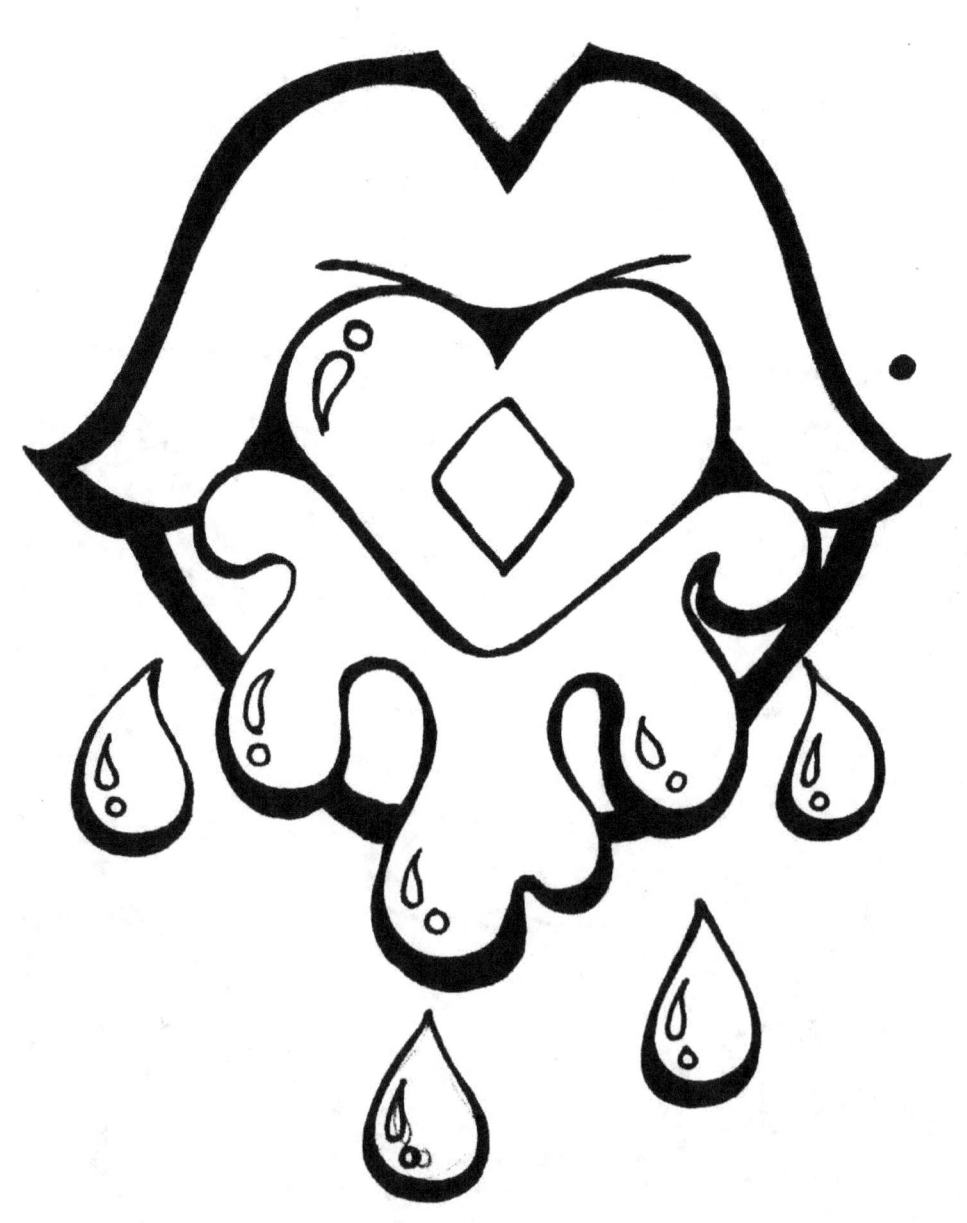

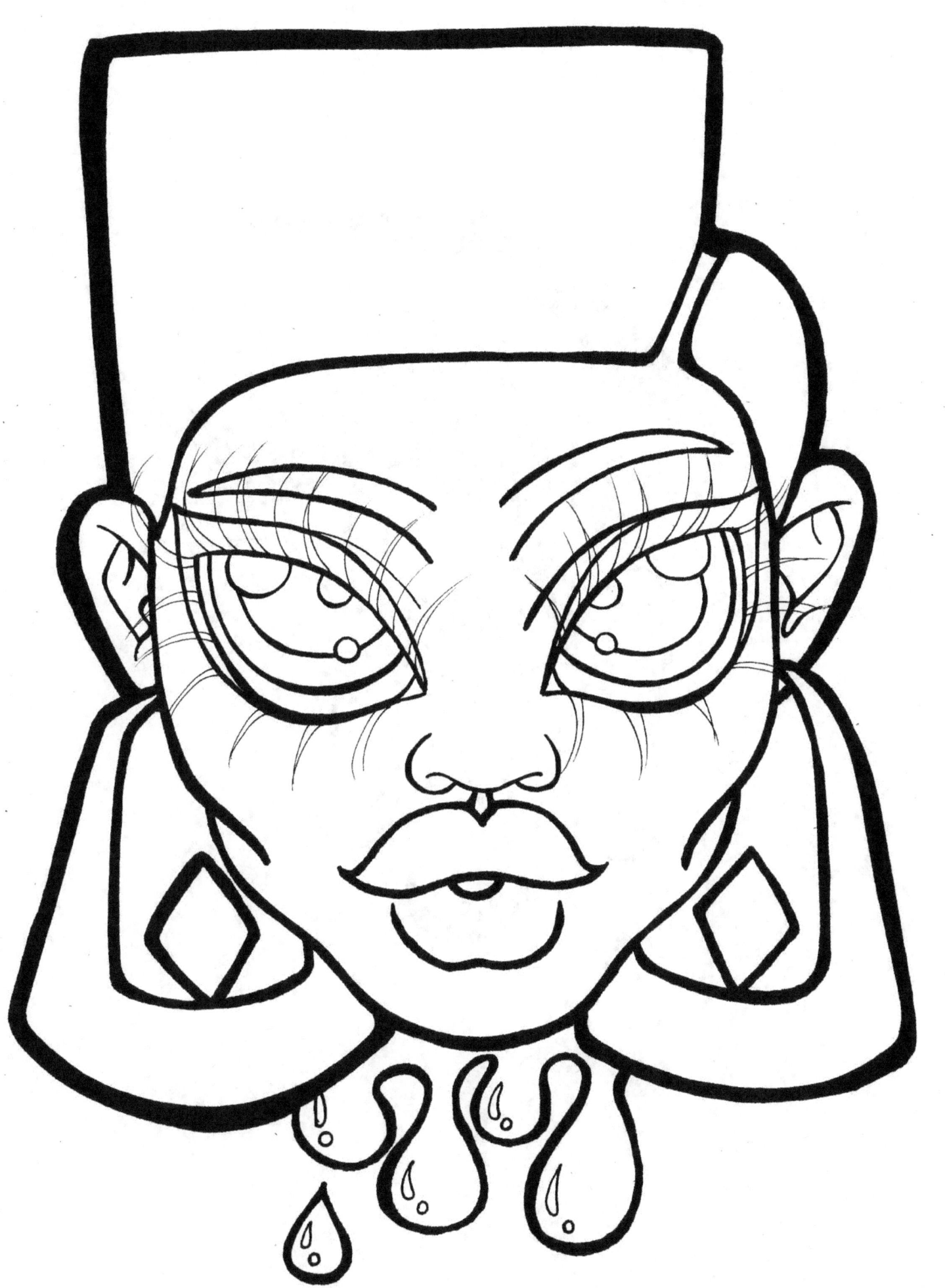

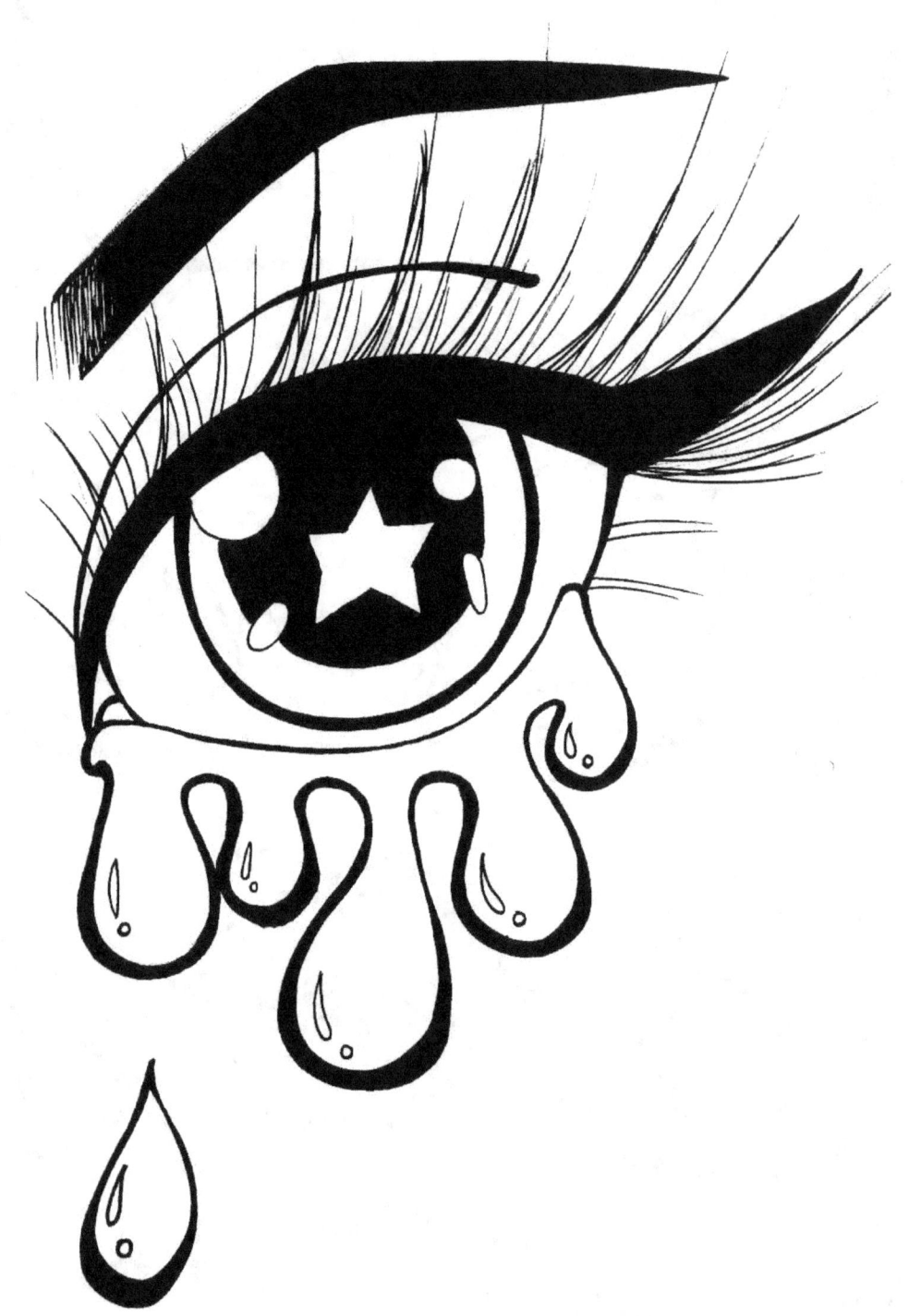

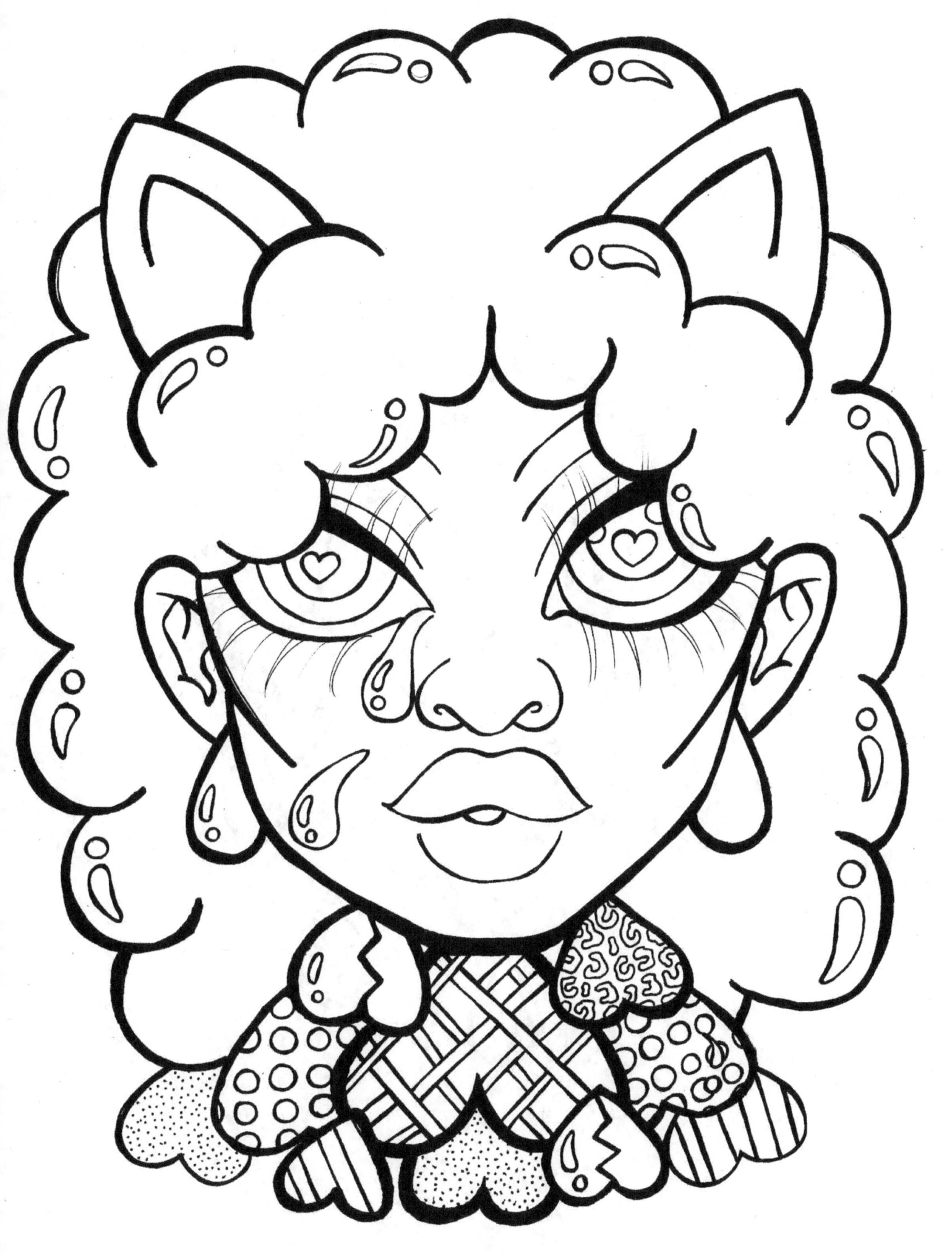

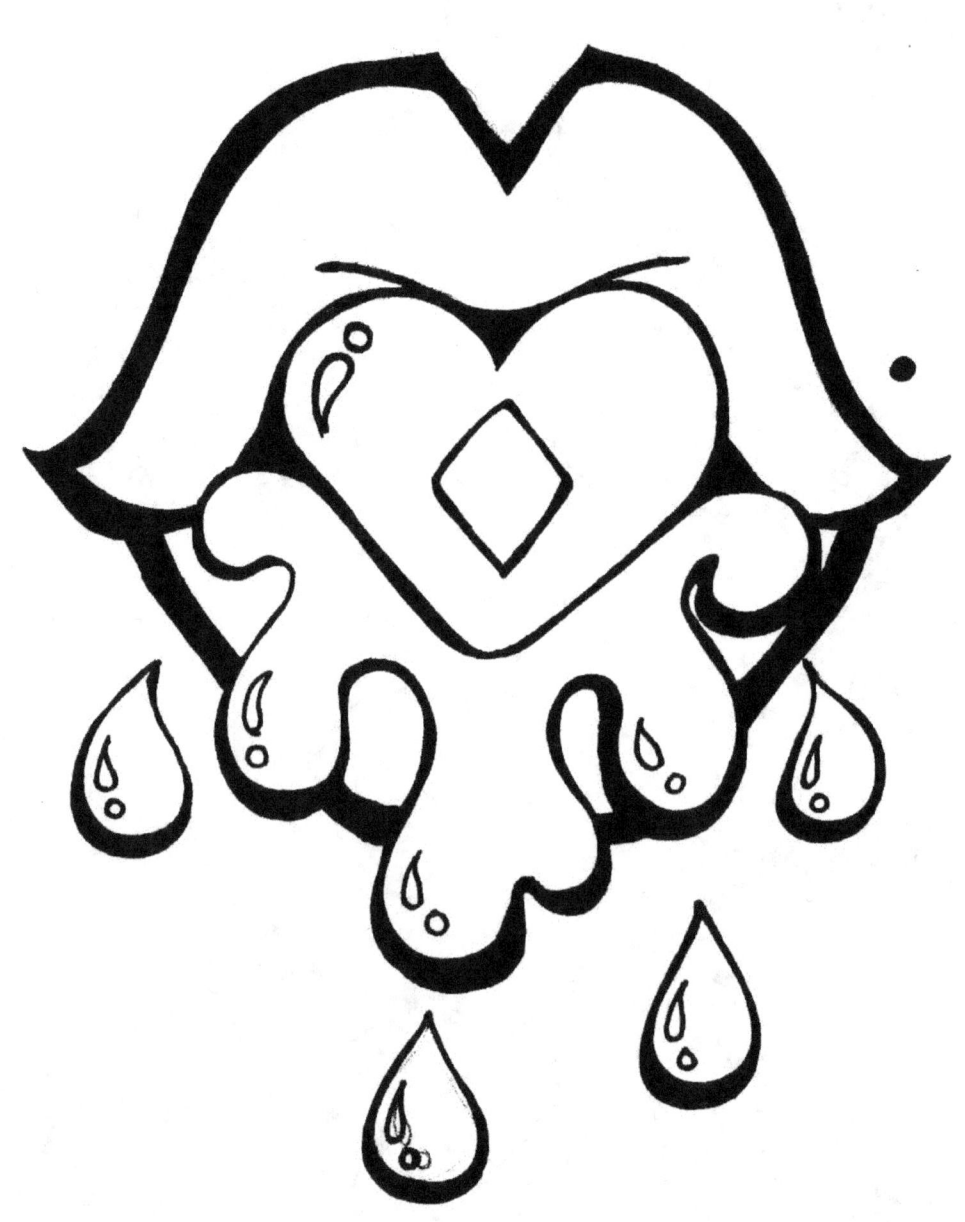

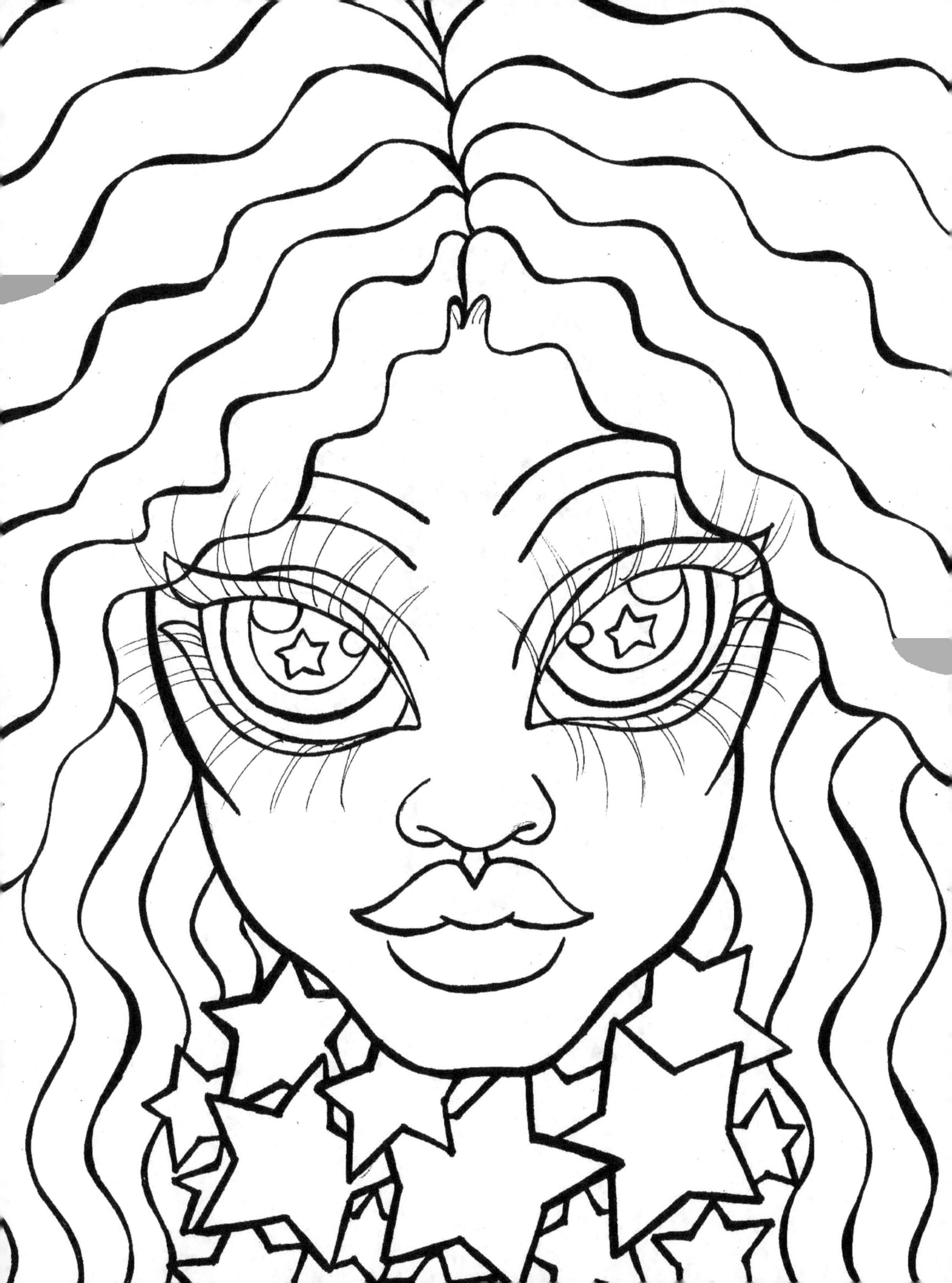

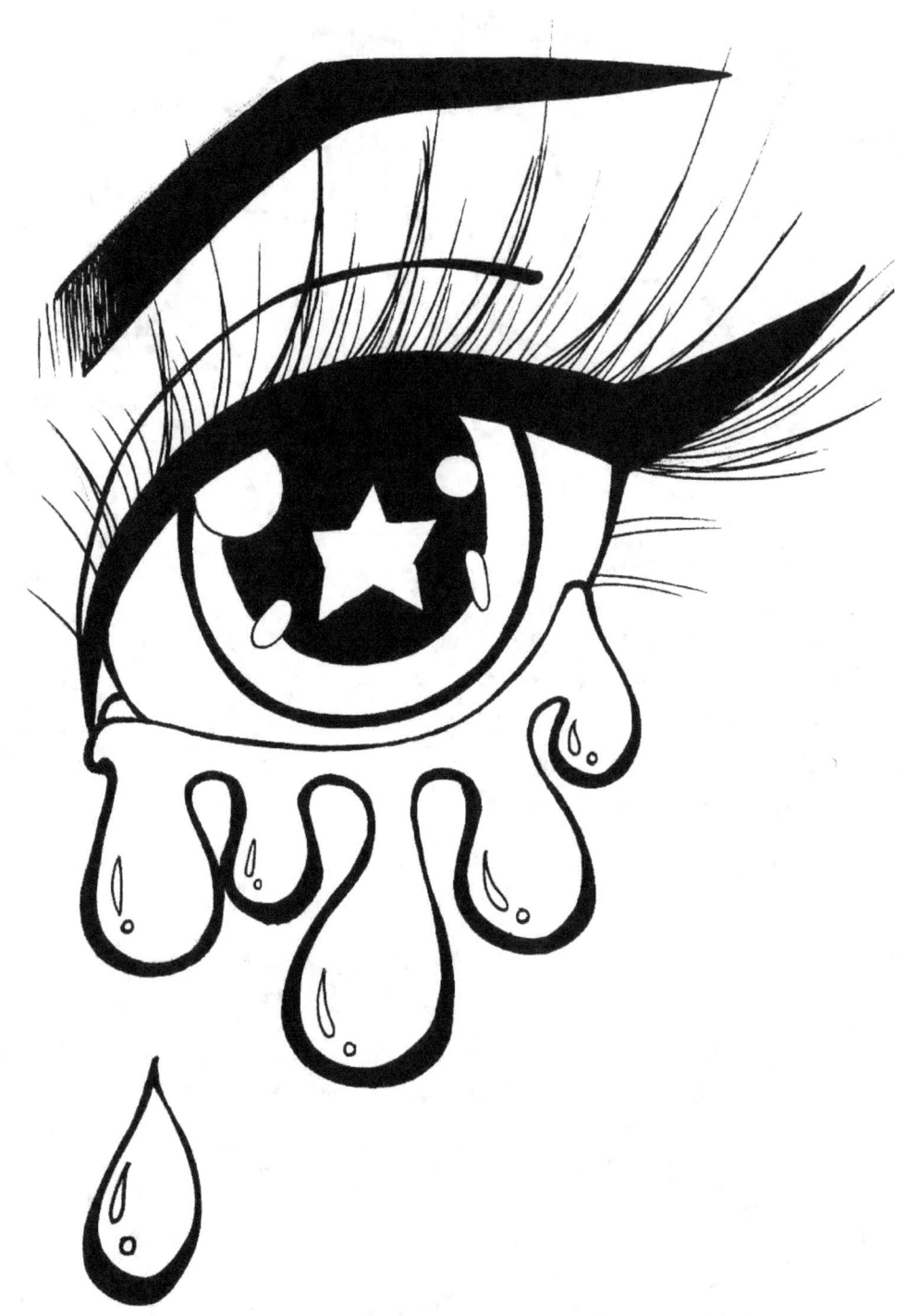

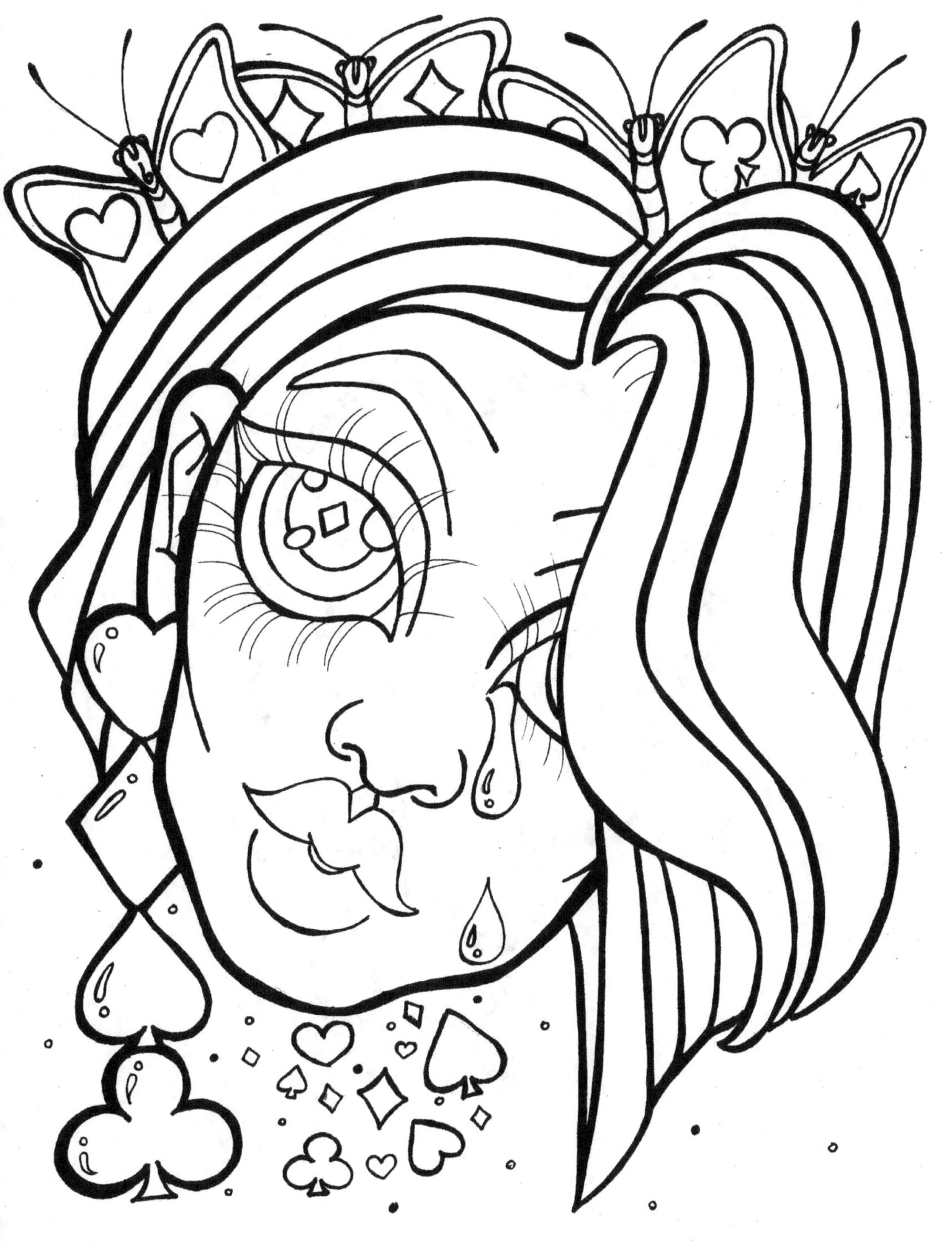

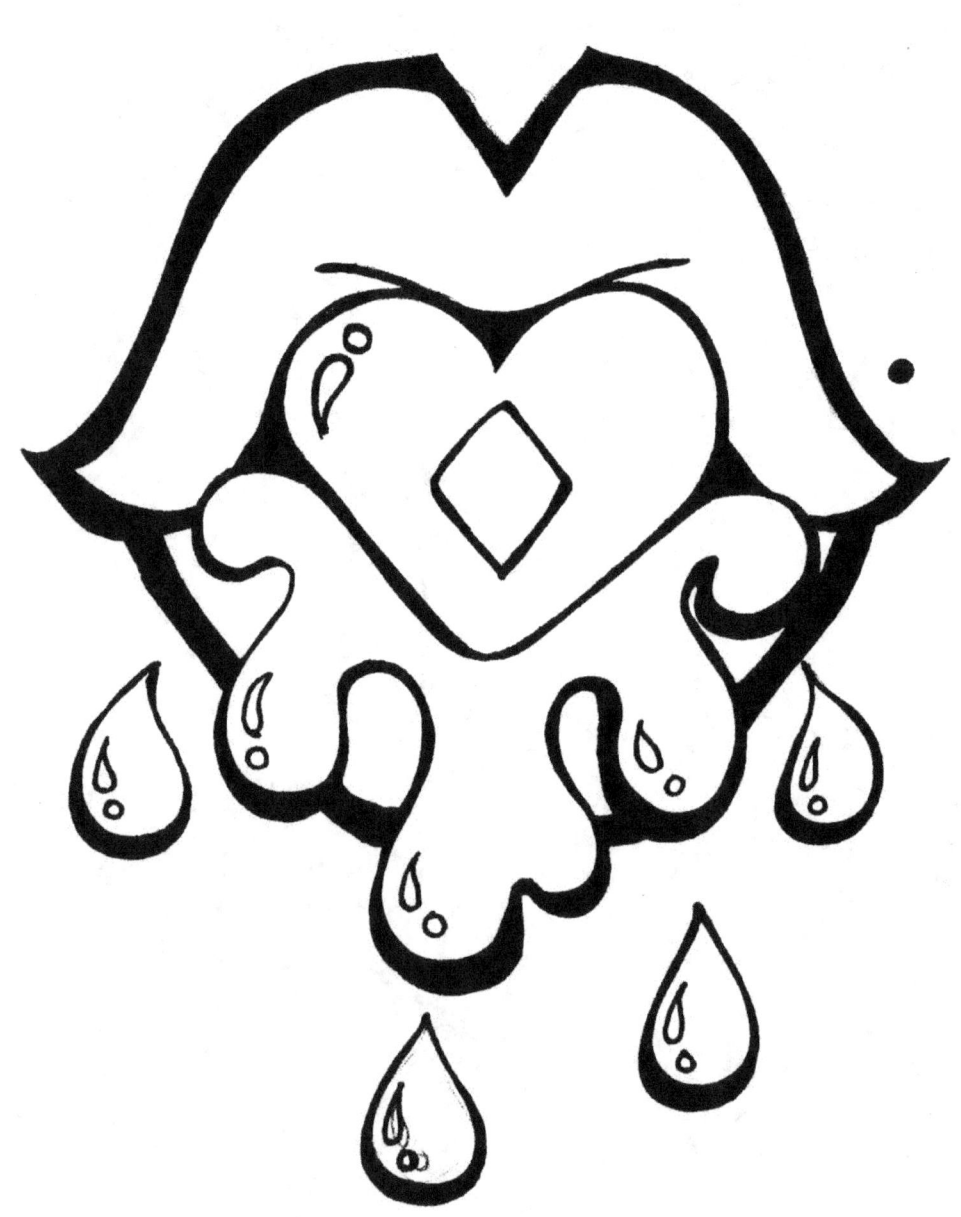

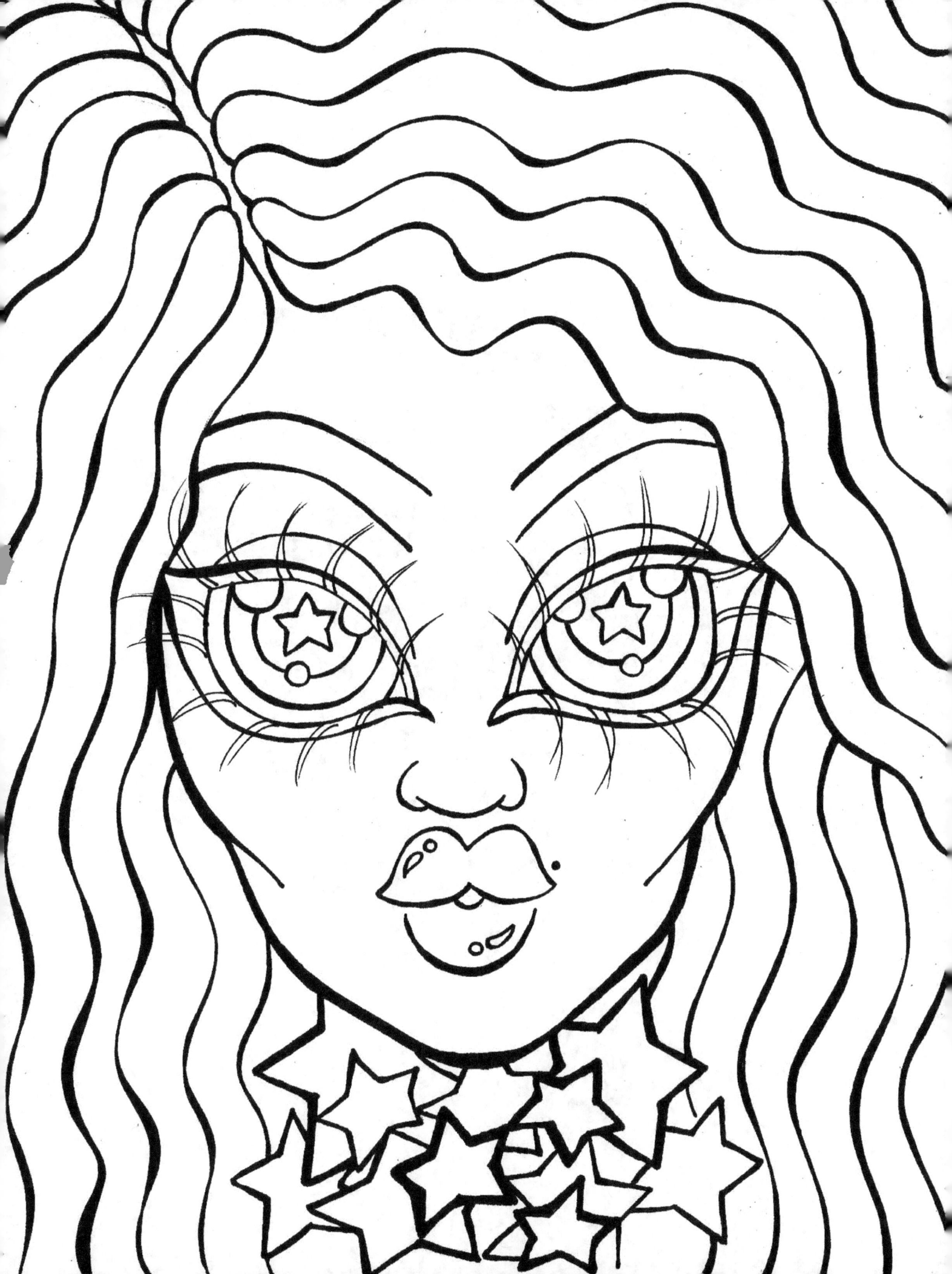

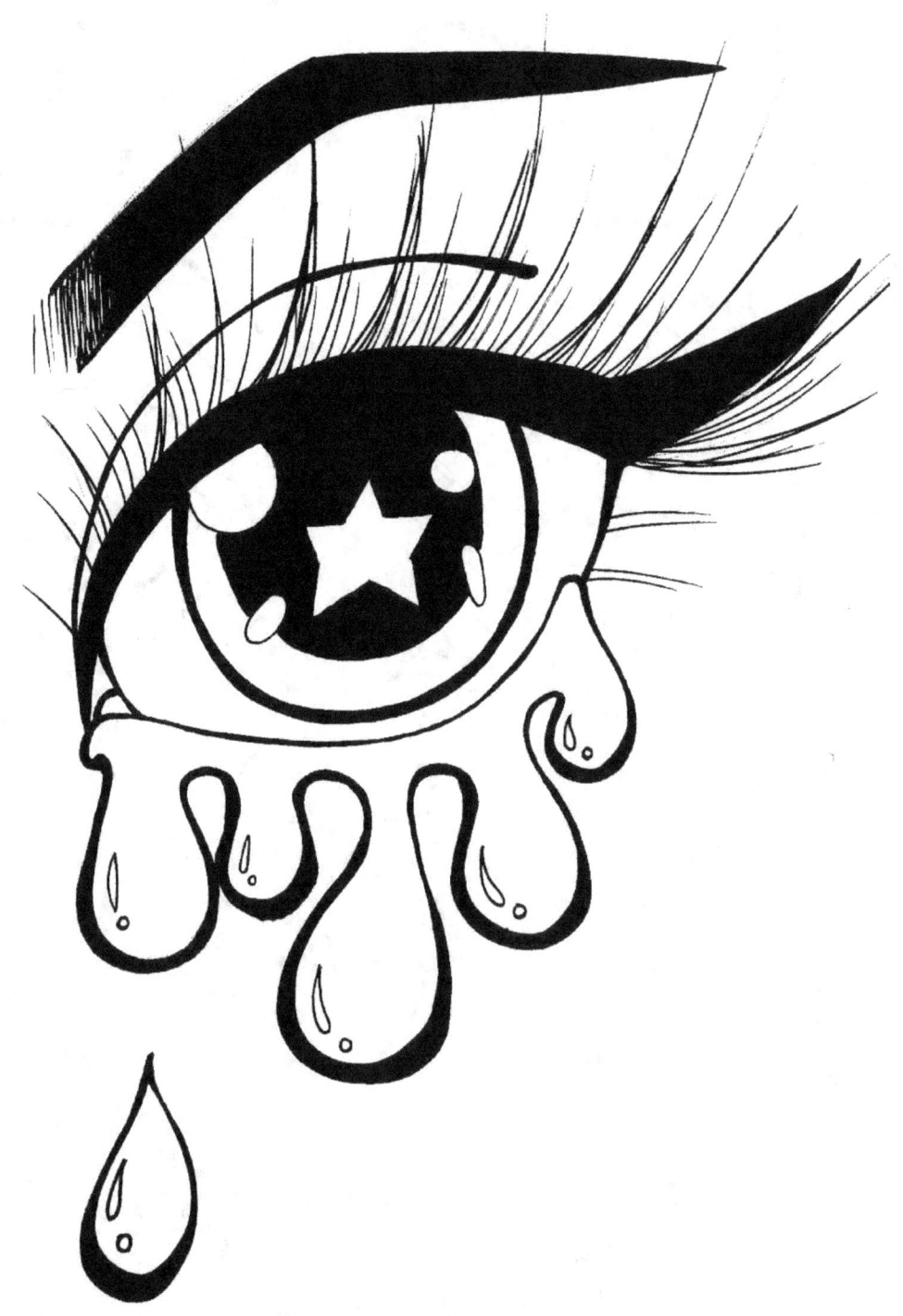

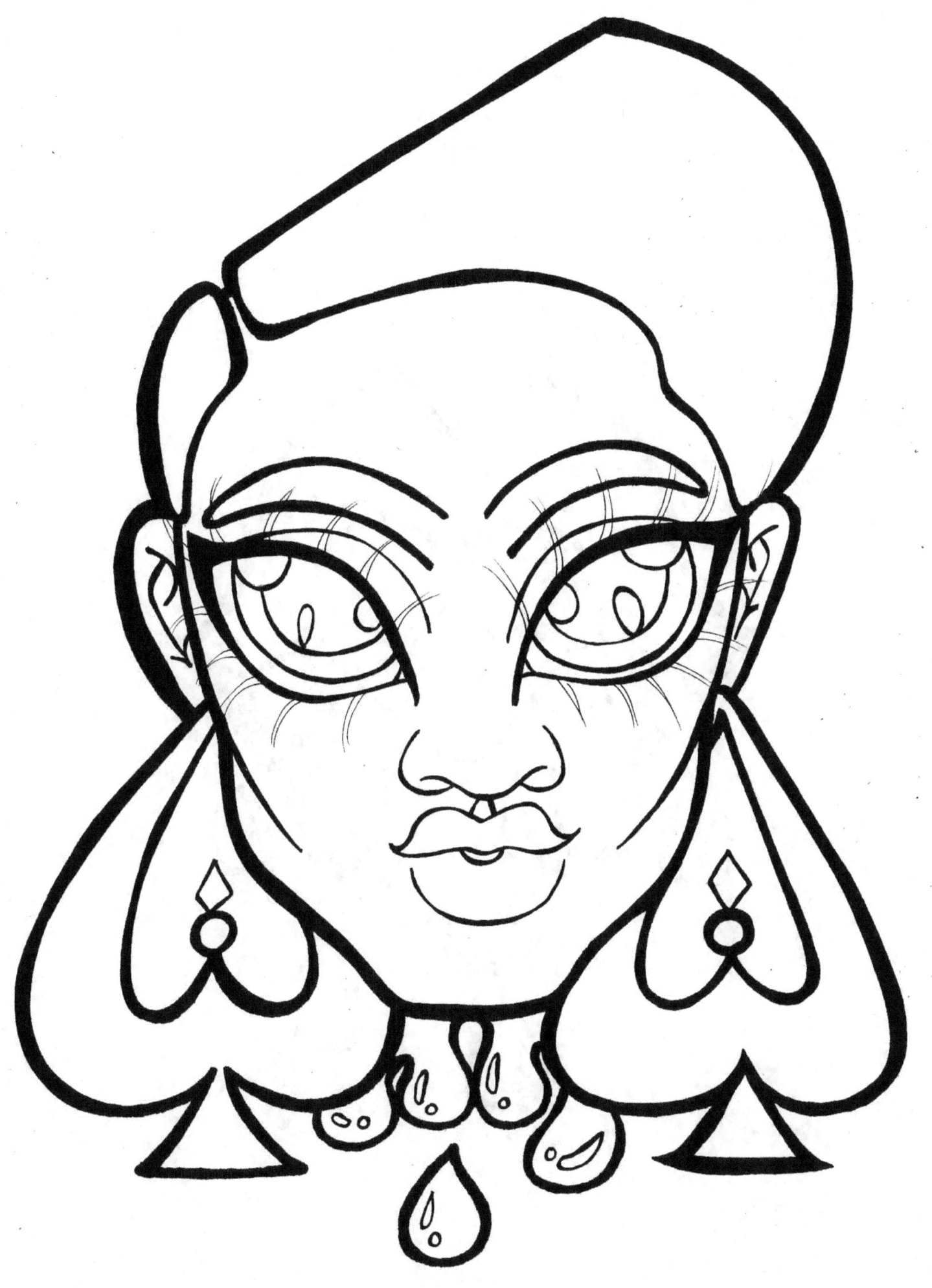

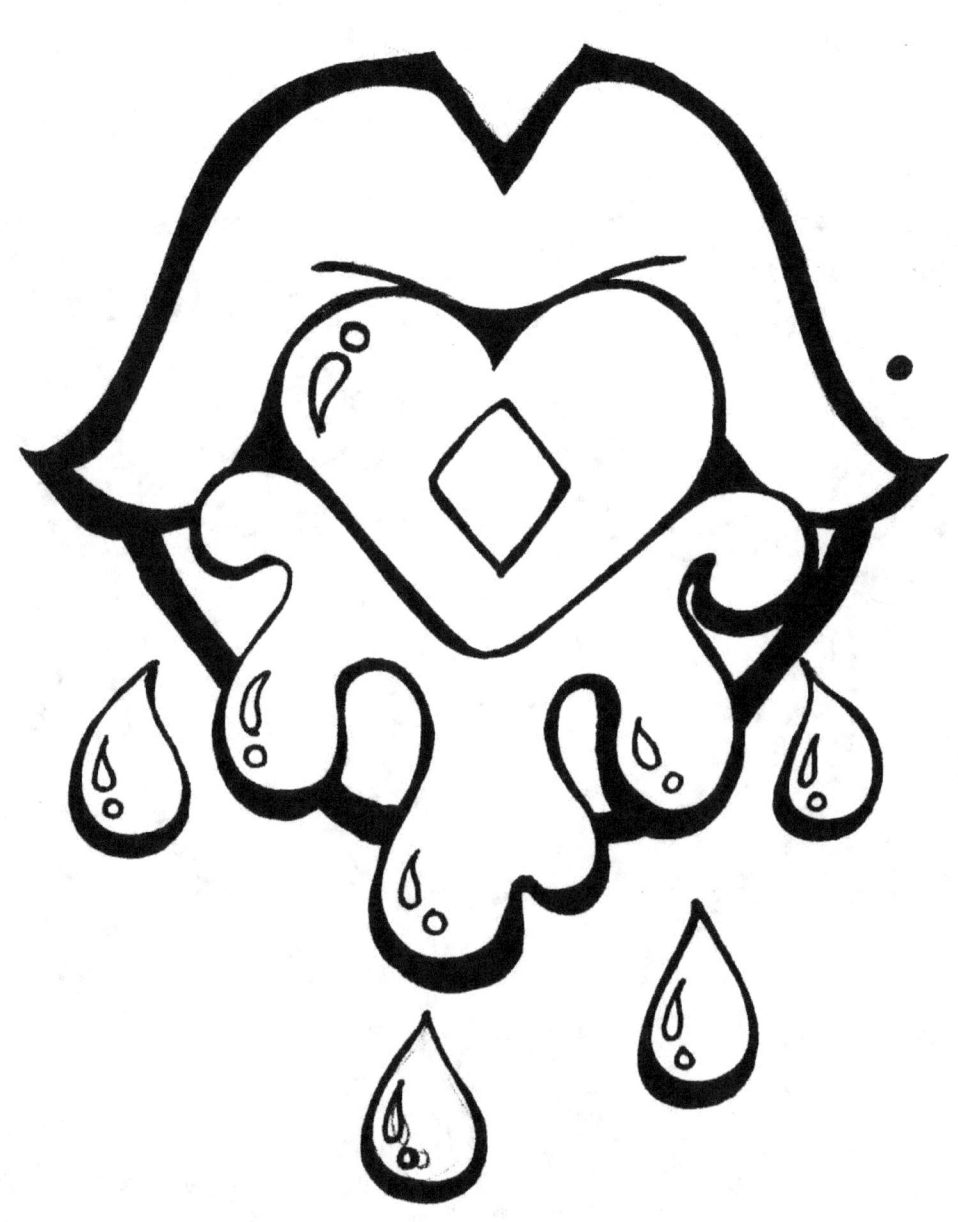

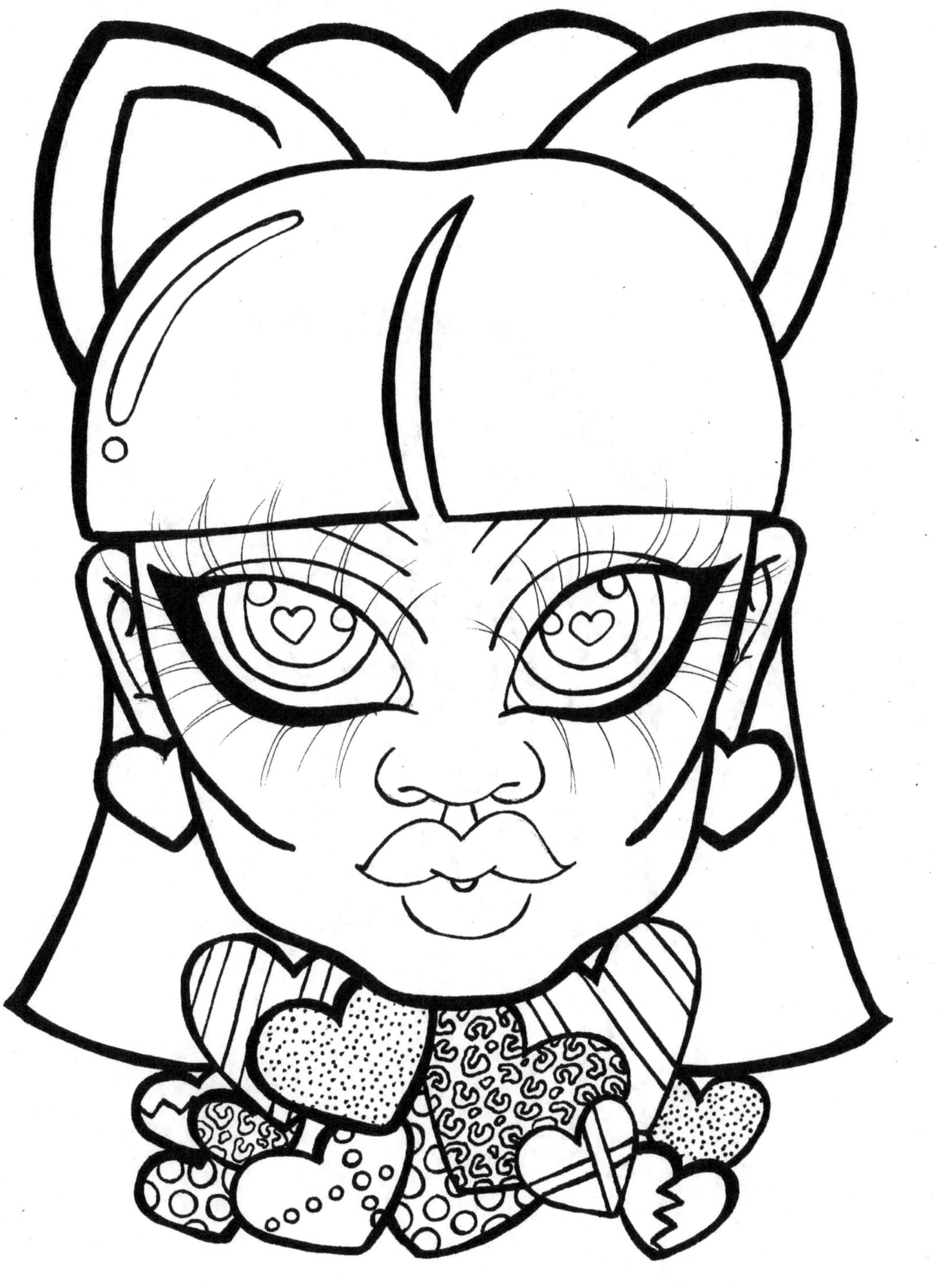

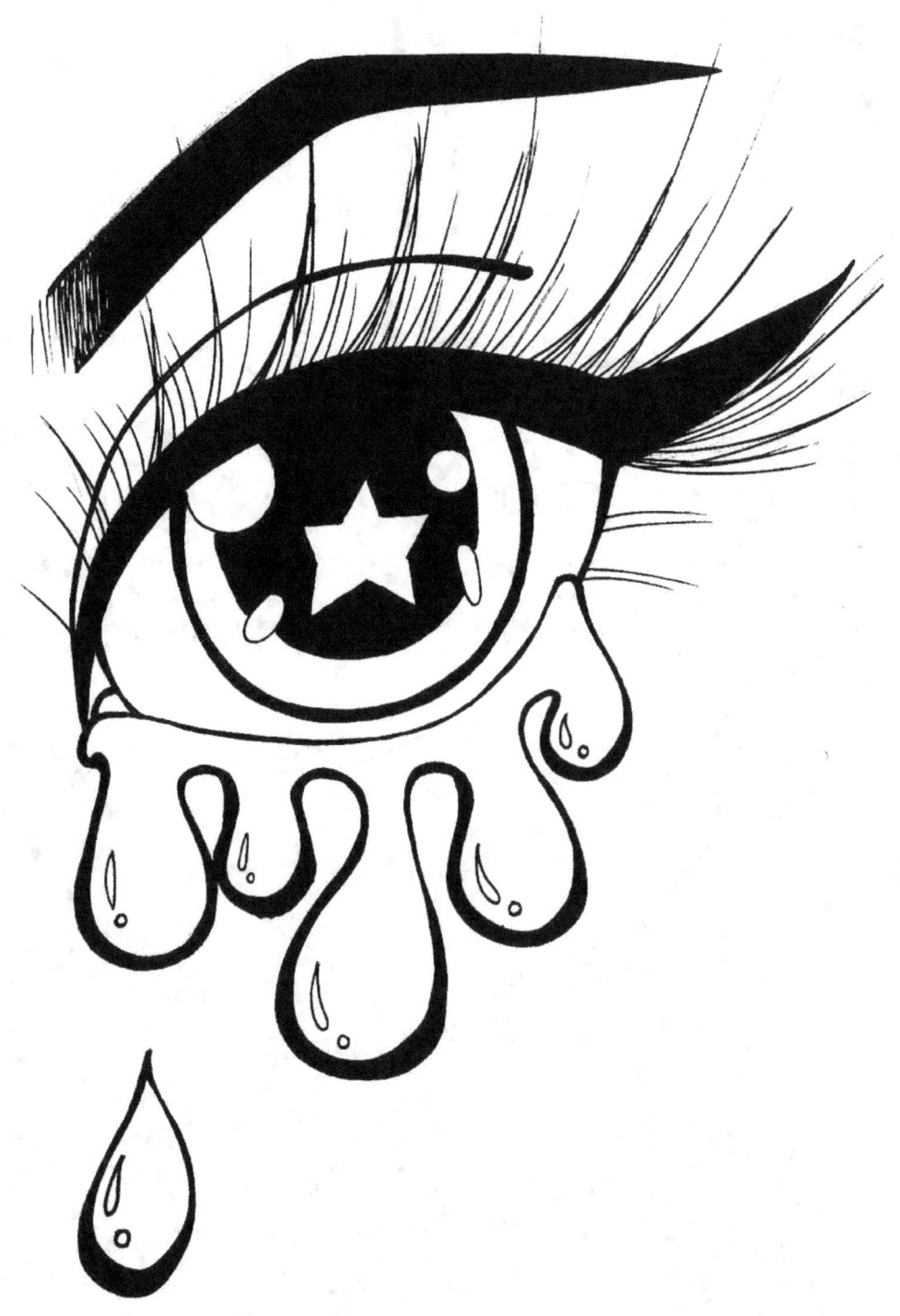

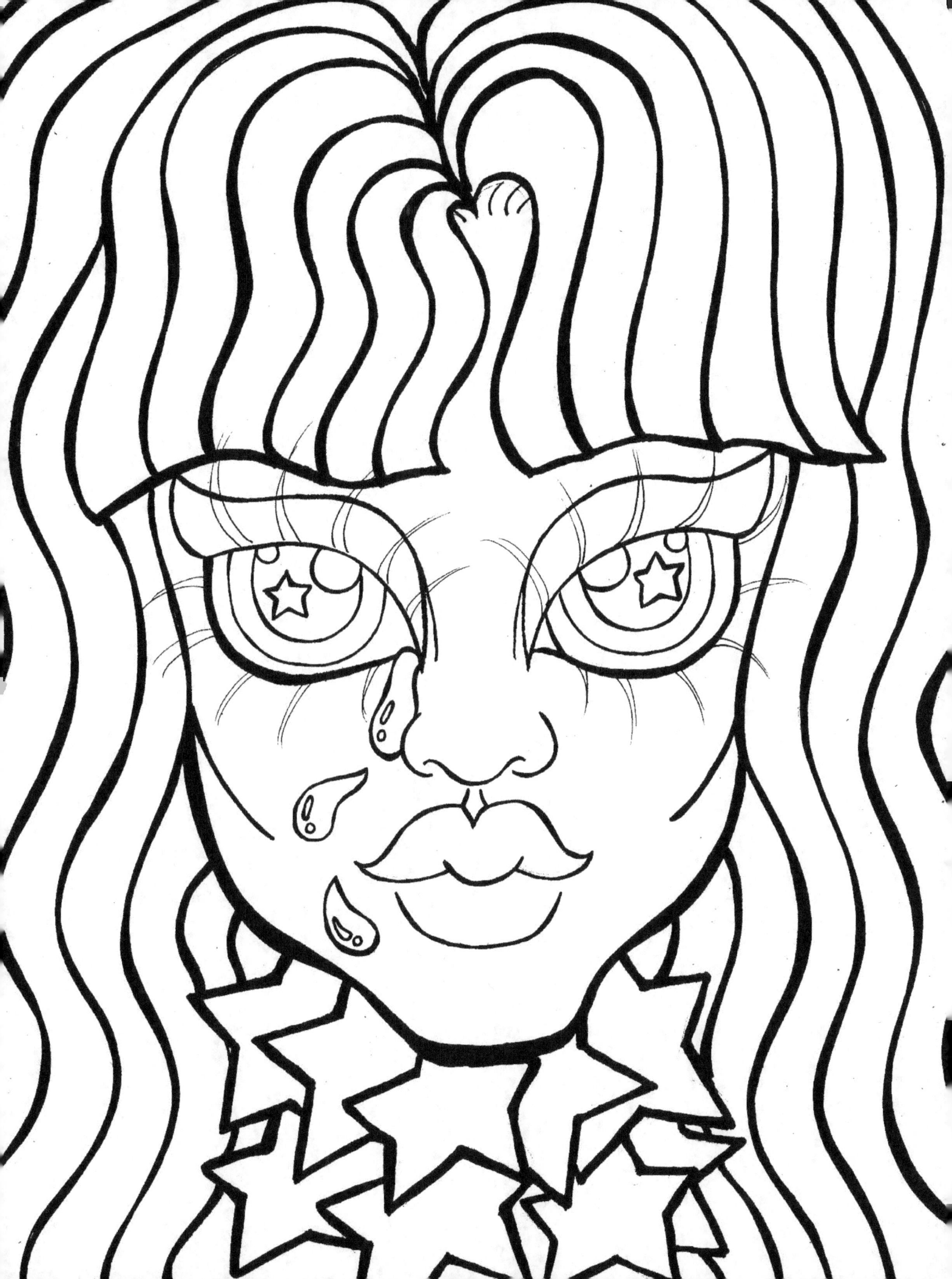

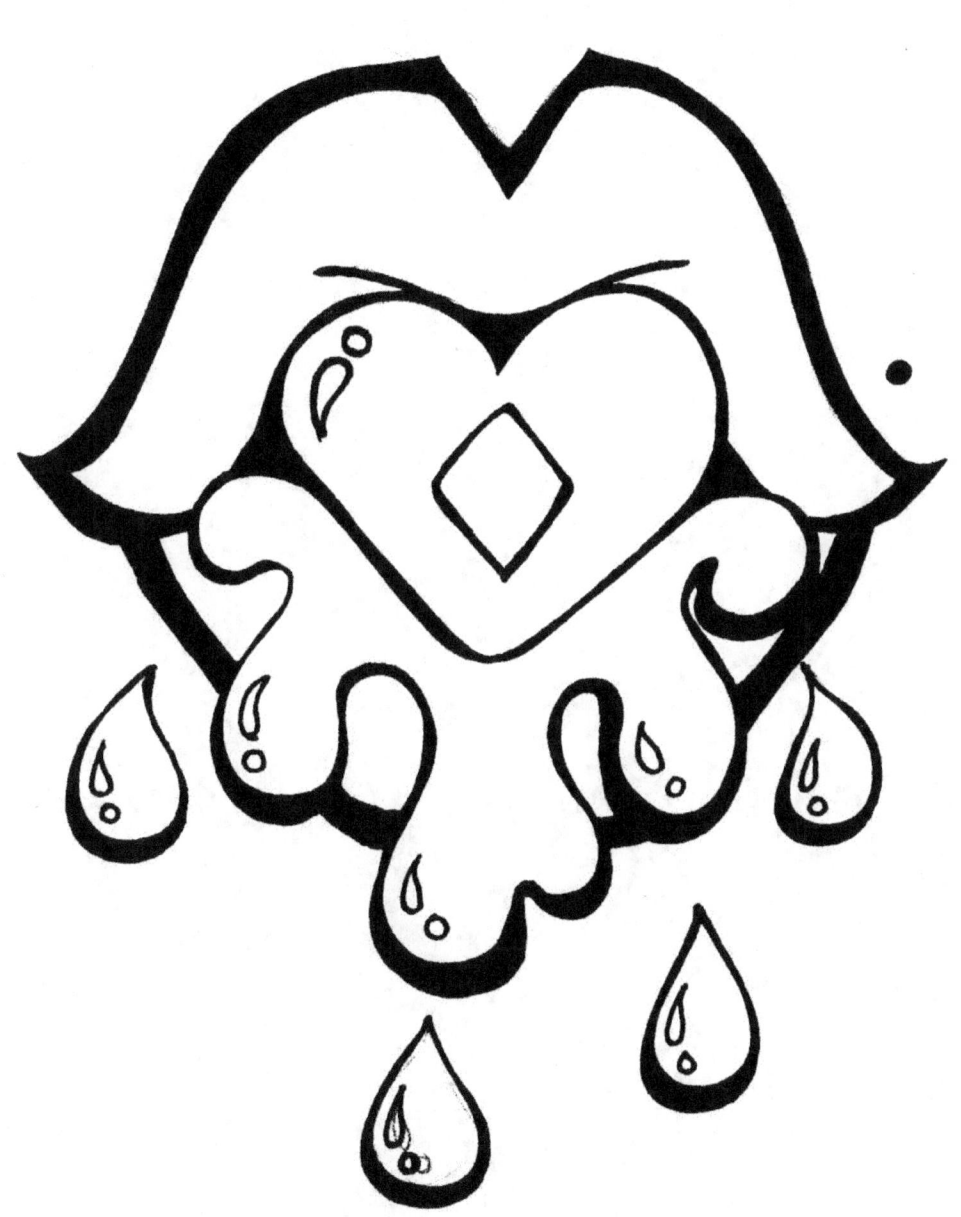

Thank you for adding Illustrious by Akeem Wayne Presents: The Beat to your coloring book collection!

Please check out other coloring books in the Illustrious Catalog:

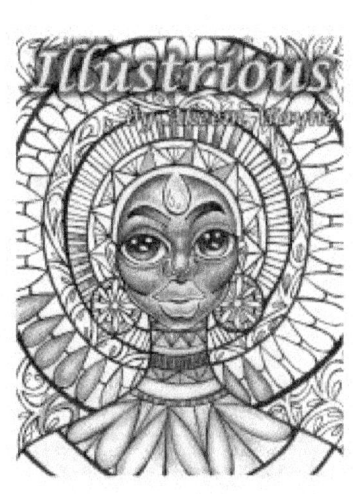
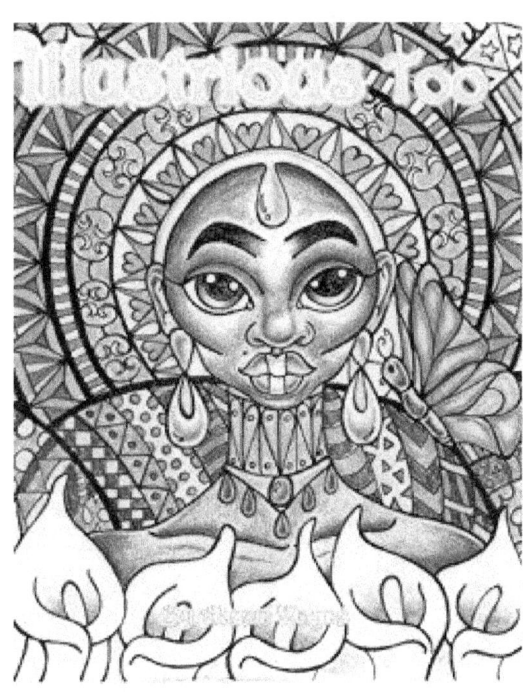
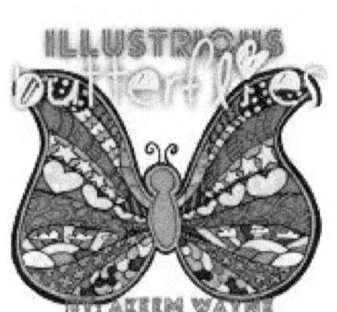
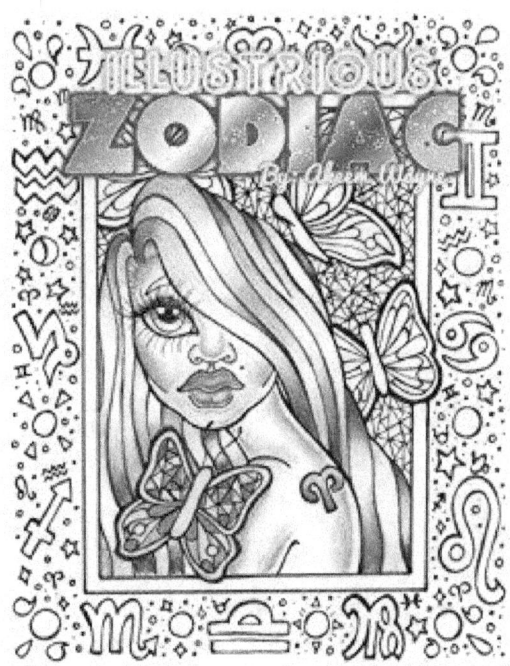

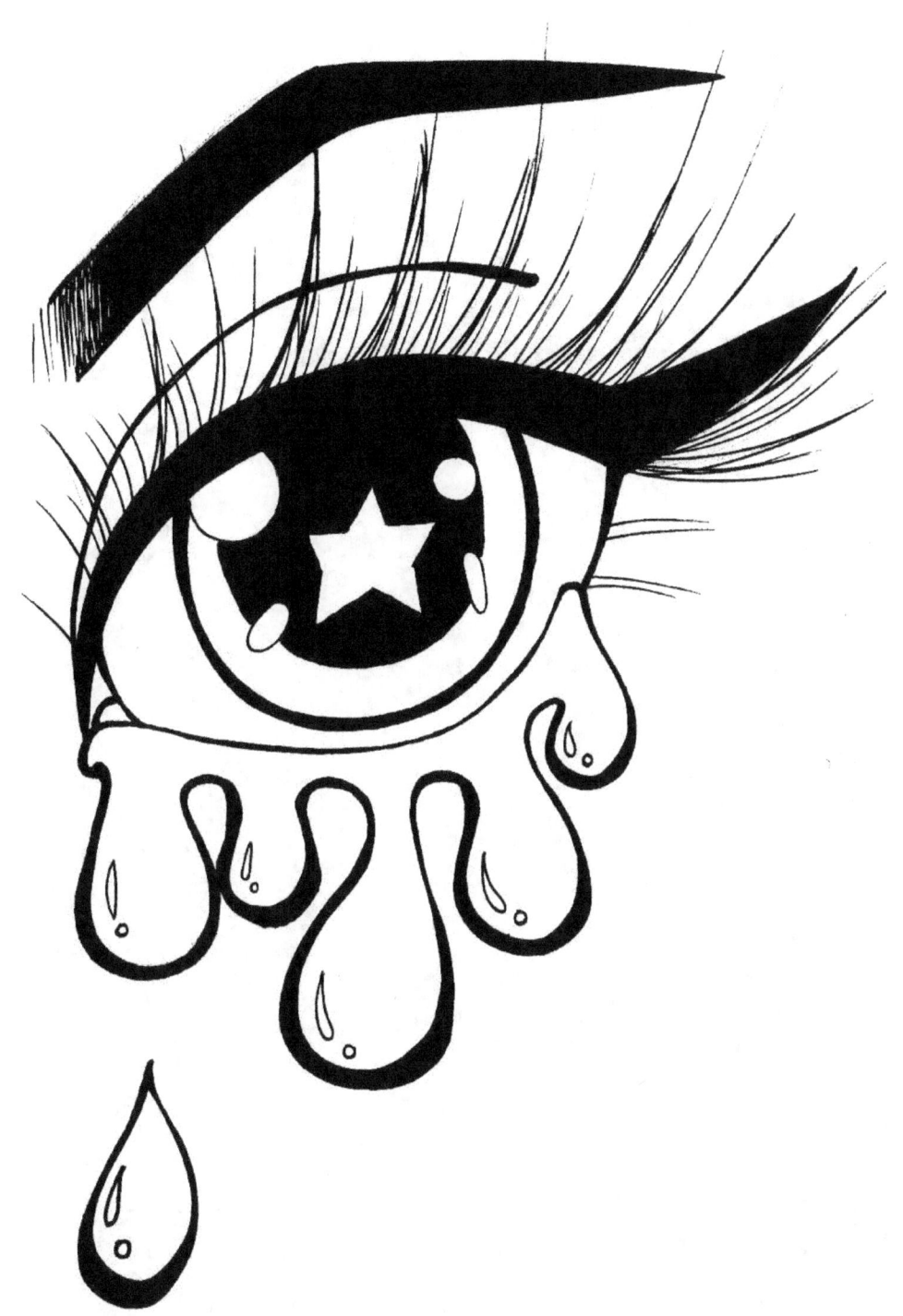

www.ingramcontent.com/pod-product-compliance
Lightning Source LLC
Chambersburg PA
CBHW062233220526
45471CB00009B/3462